Brave New Universe

PAUL J. SALVATORE

Dear Mark & Elizabeth,

With blessings & gratitude.

Paul J. Salvatore

Brave New Universe - One Man's View of All That Is
All rights reserved © 2018 Paul J. Salvatore

Front Cover Art – "Growth of Love" by Laura Davis
Back Cover Art – "Dreaming in the Right Direction" by Andrea
    Harvey
Cover Designer – Ada Frost at Kage Covers (http://adafrost.co.uk)
Editor/Formatter – Patricia Camburn Zick, The Manuscript Doctor
    (www.pczickeditor.wordpress.com)

Contact: paulsalvatore@ymail.com

ISBN-13: 978-1983773976
ISBN-10: 1983773972

DEDICATION

To my Mom and Dad, Frieda and Joseph Salvatore,
and their legacy of love

TABLE OF CONTENTS

Acknowledgments 1

Foreword 3

Introduction 6

1 Living in the Moment 9

2 The Philosophical Foundations 21

3 Losing My Religion 40

4 We're Not Gun-A Take It 60

5 A Matter of Life and Death 90

6 The Wonders of Nature 106

Epilogue – Brave New Universe 134

Resources and References 145

About the Author 151

ACKNOWLEDGMENTS

Along the path of life, we meet many, many teachers. They are not only the people who have lectured us in a classroom and given us those painful tests and homework assignments. A teacher can be young or old, weak or strong, kind or mean, smart or dull, or come in a multitude of other forms. You may find teachers to be a news reporter on TV, a musician on the radio, a coworker, or maybe even a young child quizzing a parent in the aisle of the grocery store. A teacher can be anyone we come across in life who says or does something that leaves a lasting impression on us or teaches us a lesson—be it good or bad. The better job we do of keeping our eyes and ears open, the more we will recognize them and benefit from the lessons they present to us. Therefore, I want to acknowledge all those teachers who I was blessed with along my life journey, especially those who inspired me to break down barriers, thus expanding my views on humanity and existence.

I would especially like to thank my close friend and mentor of more than forty years, Robert Vetter, for reasons that I express in this book. I would also like to recognize my dear friend, Donna Shafer, for illuminating the path of enlightenment for me in more recent years. In doing so, she has enabled me to turn my slow jog toward the light into an all-out sprint. Along the way, there were countless others who inspired and motivated me, including Dr.

Ashok Malhotra, Don Reed Simmons, Gentle Thunder, Mark Donehogawa Barfoot, the late Peter DeCaro, and Moses Starr, Jr.

Above all, I would like to acknowledge my family, especially my parents who raised their five children with love so immense, we never doubted our place in the world. Their wisdom and guidance were priceless and immeasurable. Those qualities were passed on to them from their parents, Dr. Paul and Angelina Salvatore and Theodor and Marie Wegmann. These values have become treasured heirlooms that have been passed on to all their grandchildren as well. I am grateful for all of them, and for all the joyous moments I was privileged to spend with my siblings in the loving environment my parents provided for us. No words can describe how important these things were in our upbringing, and how fortunate we are to have been shaped by such a powerful legacy of love—family is everything!

Speaking of family, I also want to acknowledge my very caring and dedicated wife, Kim, who has faithfully stood by me for more than thirty years. She is a loving wife and a mother who is practically obsessed with the well-being of our three wonderful children. They are all my teachers as well, and the ones for whom I am most grateful. I also want to give a very special thanks to my lovely and talented daughter, Diana, for volunteering her editing skills in the writing of this book, my sons, Nicolas and Daniel, for always making me want to be a better person and to my two beautiful nieces, Laura Davis and Andrea Harvey, for their inner beauty that manifests wonderfully in their fabulous artwork, some of which they were kind enough to share with me for this book.

FOREWORD

At a very young age, I fell in love with poetry and music. Whenever I would hear a beautiful song, especially one with profound and inspiring lyrics, I would feel my spirit soar to a realm far beyond the humdrum of the day's mundane events. I always loved being in that place. I always came back thankful that the world was full of such passionate people—ones who could put together such wonderful and often clever compositions. These highly inspired, transcendental artistic creations have the ability to raise the hearts, minds, and souls of humanity, at least for those who are fortunate enough to notice and appreciate them. How great it would be, I thought, to come even relatively close to having that kind of profound impact on people. But in order be able to touch someone else's soul, you must first be willing to reach deeply inwards and tap into the roots of your own soul. So, I decided to embark upon a journey toward the very core of my being in hopes of discovering any suppressed feelings and emotions and releasing them on to paper. The fruits of my labor may not be as bountiful as those of the great ones who have inspired me, but I know I am still a happier and more enriched person just for making that journey to the center of the soul.

Along the way, I have read many highly acclaimed poems and lyrics that were touted as some of the greatest ever written. While I found many of those beautiful and inspiring, other times I found myself reading lines and lines of words that hardly made any sense to me whatsoever. I'm sure the words carried deep meaning for the composers and other abstract thinkers on their frequency, but unfortunately, I was not on the same wavelength. Nonetheless, the compositions that did resonate with me sparked enough of a flame to heat up my desire to try my hand at the craft, with the goal of writing poems that most people could understand. What's the point otherwise? I originally set out to put together a pamphlet containing some of the poems I penned to share with only a small group of family and friends. I decided to take it a step further and include prose along with the poetry to explain the inspiration behind the poems. I also added many of my favorite quotes, as well as verses from sacred books of various religions to further accentuate the meaning of the topics on which I wrote. My hope is that, by taking this multi-faceted approach, it will help ensure that most readers will not only understand the meaning in *all* of the poetic compositions but also feel moved or inspired by my elaborations on their meaning. I hope you will enjoy them for what they are, and take with you whatever you find valuable. You will notice that I dare to write about some very controversial and emotionally charged topics, which are usually topics that invoke great passion. Passion is what provides good inspiration for composing poetry and literature. However, passion often clashes with reason. Keep that thought in the back of your mind as you read on, and exercise your free will to make your own determinations. Although I strive not to be judgmental, I also believe it is human nature to formulate opinions, but opinions can be changed if we are open to new information.

I also wanted to share some of my life experiences and scholastic endeavors that I delved into over the years, which have had a profound impact on how I view the world and "all that is." I especially want to credit all the people who have entered my life and done the same, whether by the books they wrote, the songs they composed, the quotes they uttered, or by my direct interaction with them. I hope by sharing these insights, you will feel some of the same joy and inspiration that found its way into my life and helped me to grow and evolve toward enlightenment. I also hope you will feel inclined to share some of these visions with others, especially if you think it will help them with whatever they may be experiencing at a particular time in their life. The act of sharing brings joy in and of itself. Above all, I hope this book can help send out a message of unity and remind people that we are all passengers on the same "spaceship" revolving around our sun.

INTRODUCTION

When I was a younger man in my late twenties, I decided to read the book, *Brave New World*, which I had wanted to read for a long time but never found the time. I am glad that I finally made the time to read it because of the lasting impression it left on me, and how it inspired some of my subsequent writings, including the title of this book and some of its contents. The author of *Brave New World*, Aldous Huxley, was a brilliant man who was known for many things besides author, including a humanist, pacifist, and satirist. He also took interest in subjects that I also have a genuine interest in, including parapsychology, mysticism, and a philosophical and theological concept known as universalism. To my understanding, universalism embraces the notion that some ideas, including those of various religions and other belief systems, have universal application. It also supports the idea that parallels can be drawn between different schools of thought to formulate a synergistic, universal world view. This notion of acceptance and reconcilement of different philosophies, religions, and schools of thought is very appealing to me and consistent with my own personal views on both the natural world and the divine, which I had already developed and embraced prior to reading *Brave New World* and learning more about Huxley.

Brave New World left me with a strong impression that we should be wary of both technology and the tendency to conform to strict structures, lest we become progressively more dehumanized. The book depicts a bleak future wherein humanity has become almost completely industrialized and is controlled by a small group of elite rulers. Almost all humans in this fictitious society are genetically programmed to fulfil specific, predetermined roles and are mass-produced in laboratories. The natural processes of birth, aging, and death are viewed as horrors in this world and are looked upon with disgust, so people are required to stay medicated on a drug called *soma* to help them remain content and cope with life in this dystopic society. The rulers are aware of the shortcomings of this type of tightly controlled society, but they consider the loss of freedom and individuality to be a small price to pay for maintaining stability.

Aside from the people who were mass-produced in laboratories, there were others who came into the world through the natural birth process, such as the character John, who was referred to as "the Savage." John was removed from a Savage Reservation in New Mexico and introduced to the dystopian society described in the book, the setting of which is futuristic London, England. I associated John, and his dilemma described in this disturbing setting, with our modern day Native Americans and the trials and tribulations they faced, and still face, in post-Columbus American society where they were forced to learn English, adopt Christianity, and otherwise conform to the ways of the invading settlers who eventually confined them to reservations.

The scenario depicted in *Brave New World* may seem far-fetched, but when you think of recent developments in genetic engineering, artificial intelligence, unprecedented corporate power, and attempted movements toward a New World Order, it should at least give some reason for concern and suspicion about where our current society may be heading. It is important to note that Huxley wrote *Brave New* World in 1932, long before any of these developments. With that sobering thought in mind, I now share with you some of my own views and compositions on the topics of philosophy, religion, politics, society, the natural world, and a variety of other matters of human interest.

CHAPTER ONE
LIVING IN THE MOMENT

The past is dead, and the future is just imagined.

This phrase is perhaps my all-time favorite. Every day I find it to be one of the most helpful and useful to me. I first heard it uttered by a good friend and former college roommate, and it is a concept we both learned a lot about in college while dabbling in various schools of philosophical thought during our studies. It was derived from a quote by Ken Keyes, Jr., which is, *"The past is dead. The future is imaginary. Happiness can only be in the eternal now moment."* The concept is simple—just be present in the here and now. It's a mantra that's been advocated throughout history in various cultures and belief systems all around the world.

In Buddhism, for instance, it is believed that true happiness and contentment can be attained, and suffering avoided, if we just give up useless craving and learn to live our lives *one day at a time* not dwelling on past events or ones yet to come. Adopting this perspective also leaves us with more free time and energy to devote to helping others. In turn, we would be rewarded with a sense of happiness, fulfilment, and freedom that Buddhists refer to as nirvana.

I am willing to bet that some readers may have drifted off right away by reading about some unfamiliar Eastern school of thought—one that may be radically different than how you were raised, and one that you might even consider to be weird. For a moment, let's just say that the terms Buddhist and nirvana are nothing more than just names or labels.

Perhaps if the points I made earlier about the beliefs of Buddhism did not actually include the terms "Buddhism" or "nirvana," many people might be more receptive to the concept. Let's try a little experiment to prove my point. If you happen to be Christian, go back and read that paragraph again and substitute the words "Buddhism" and "Buddhists" with "Christianity" and "Christians" and the word "nirvana" with the phrase "finding Jesus." I bet it works for you. You may even want to reference Matthew 6:34, which states, *"Therefore do not worry about tomorrow, for tomorrow will worry about itself. Each day has enough trouble of its own."*

So, you're an atheist and don't want to hear about any religion at all? Then try using the words "atheism/atheists" and "contentment" as your substitutes instead. It will probably work for you as well.

In my experience, I have found that there seems to be a natural tendency, even if just subconscious, for us to evaluate and interpret information about other cultures, religions, and belief systems through the filters of our own. This is something that I most definitely have been guilty of myself countless times. It is a tendency that I now try to keep in check the best I can. What a better place the world would be if we spent more time and energy looking for all that we have in common with others, rather than fearing those who don't label themselves the same as we do! Over the course of my lifetime, I have developed an aversion to naming and labeling in general, because I believe by doing so we create artificial barriers and roadblocks to understanding. I also believe labeling fosters intolerance of different perspectives by painting people into a corner. This phenomenon will be elaborated upon later, so let's get back to the present.

To put the present in perspective, we must also consider the past and the future.

"Those who cannot remember the past are condemned to repeat it."

~ George Santayana

Nothing can be done to change the past, but we would all be fools if we did not make a point to learn from it. Put another way, those who fail to learn from history are doomed to relive it and repeat over and over again, all the bad mistakes made by those who came before us. However, although the past should not be forgotten, neither should it be *dwelled* upon, lest we may also be doomed to sink in its quicksand and be completely consumed by those bad memories. Clinging onto them will eat away at us like a cancer if we don't just let them go.

Abandon Ship

I once wrestled with this yearning
And it had me burning mad
Stumbling over shadows
Of the things I could have had
But my life I couldn't salvage
And my course I couldn't find
Until I cut away the anchors;
Left those sinking ships behind

"You build on failure. You use it as a stepping stone. Close the door on the past. You don't try to forget the mistakes, but you don't dwell on it. You don't let it have any of your time, or any of your space."

~ Johnny Cash

At the same time, it doesn't do us any good to worry about what might happen in the days to come. Living the life of a worry-wart can lead us down the dark and dreary path of mental distress, anxiety, or perhaps even worse. Some people may torture themselves so severely with anxiety about what might happen in the future that it could literally drive them insane. In some cases, the oppression of clinging too tightly to the past or stressing too much about the future could lead to a life marred by a host of problems, including health issues, drug and alcohol addiction, relationship problems, despair, or perhaps even depression or suicide. The list of possible maladies and forms of suffering that can be caused by straying from the here and now is exhausting, so why torture ourselves? Life is too short and precious! I came to the realization that I was a victim to some of these maladies myself after landing up in the hospital with stress-related conditions in my forties and early fifties. Fortunately, I was successful in getting those conditions under control by adopting a major shift in lifestyle and perspective. I let go of most of the materialistic concerns that gained a dangerous grip on me and returned to the more spiritual practices of meditation, yoga, and Qui Gong I had participated in earlier in life to help keep me focused on the here and now.

Days to Come

What is going to happen? How I wish I knew
What the future holds for me; just give me a clue
How high will I climb or how hard will I fall?
Oh, how I just wish I had a magic crystal ball

Will I be a hero, or will I be a dud?
The puzzled local psychic said it's clear as mud
Who will be my soulmate—a pauper or a queen?
Think I'll just go buy myself a fancy time machine

He's keeping it a secret, shrewd old Father Time
Mocking me for asking—as if it were a crime
To think about the days to come, every day and night
Incessantly lamenting about my lack of second sight

Funny how it happens—it creeps up on you fast
Those days I wasted searching are now days of future passed
As I lay here on my death bed, being drawn into the light,
I only wish I had the chance to go back and get it right

"Life is what happens to us while we are making other plans."

~ Allen Saunders

If the past is truly dead, and the future is only imagined, that leaves us with nothing but the present. If you stop and think about it, that's all there *really* is for us to experience. All our past experiences and visions of the future exist only in our minds. So, let's learn from the past, have some hopes for our future, but not make ourselves a slave to or victim of either one. If we just gently bob around life's obstacles like a cork in a stream, rather than struggling to swim upstream or careening into the rocks downstream, it will make our lives a lot simpler. Besides, I don't think anyone will argue with the notion that life offers plenty for us to focus on right NOW.

"What lies behind us and what lies before us are tiny matters compared to what lies within us."

~ Ralph Waldo Emerson

Now or Never

The past is dead and something
That was meant to leave behind
And the future's just a seedling
In the corners of our mind
Living in another time
Will lead your life astray
Be here now or be aware
You'll never find your way

"Learn from yesterday, live for today, hope for tomorrow. The important thing is not to stop questioning."

~ Albert Einstein

car·pe di·em [*English* **kahr**-pey **dee**-*uh* m] *Latin.* Seize the day; enjoy the present, as opposed to placing all hope in the future.

The clock is ticking, and there is no "pause" button we can press to put our lives on hold. Again, I regress back to my college days like they were yesterday, and I recall having to perform an oral interpretation assignment for one of my language arts classes. I chose to recite the lyrics to the song "Time" by Pink Floyd. I first heard that song as a very young man in the early 1970s and, to this day, it still sends a shiver up my spine listening to the words. The song warns about how time can creep up on you and how you may suddenly realize that ten years have quickly passed. A sobering thought for me is that more than four decades have passed since I first heard the song, and those foreboding words had impacted me even the first time I ever heard them, as young as I was! Sometimes we need something to snap us back into reality and remind us that we don't have forever to take care of everything on our "bucket list." Procrastination is a tenacious enemy—a cunning culprit that sneaks up on us and robs us of our precious time—but only if we let it have its dastardly way with us.

Although I am grateful for all the accomplishments I have achieved in my life thus far, I still must try hard not to think about all the lost opportunities—all those wonderful things I know I could have experienced and accomplished had I only made a point to "seize the day." No regrets, though—the past is dead— just keep moving forward.

Chains of Time

Childhood dreams had left my head
I couldn't fathom what was said
The magic feeling turned to dread
Childhood dreams had left my head

My favorite song was never played
The loveliest music ever made
The sun was beaming rays of shade
My favorite song was never played

The love I knew had turned on me
A day I thought would never be
Our castle was too near the sea
The love I knew had turned on me

Glad I left it all behind
Slipping loose from chains of time
Turn the page or lose your mind
Glad I left it all behind!

By the way, seizing the day does not always involve an ambitious activity, like getting that closet cleaned out, seeing more patients, or getting more contracts signed. It could mean putting all that business aside for a moment and treating yourself to some much-needed time to kick back and savor the simple pleasures in life. Perhaps you should spend some quality time enjoying the company of your family and friends. Maybe just go outside for a walk and sit yourself down by the edge of a pond where you can gaze off into nature and listen to those crickets and birds chirp for a while. Depending on your situation, that may very well be the best thing you can do to seize the day and make the best use of your time; just what the doctor ordered.

"It's time! No more floundering in the deadly riptide of procrastination. You'll be clobbered all the harder by the boomerang of time, the farther you try to toss it."

One First Step

One short call, he's got the job
He packs his things to go
Someone's working in his chair—
He moved his tail too slow

One quick glance ignites a flame
That's washed out just as fast
Reflections of her diamond ring
On broken hearts they splash

One first shot begins a war
Forever shall it rage
Their hands can write the book of peace,
But their pride can't turn the page

One first step is all it takes
To get us on our way
Get in tune and strike a beat—
The band's begun to play

One of those who inspired me to strike while the iron is hot and not to pass up the myriad of opportunities that life presents to us daily was my brother, John. One day, he very spontaneously decided to cut school and pursue his lifelong dream of becoming an entertainer by venturing into New York City to audition for a Broadway show. Thus, began his long and prosperous career as a Broadway performer and a world-class entertainer. It was a long, hard road he traveled leading up to that fateful day; not all days were bright and sunny. Sometimes, we really need to just suck it up and persevere through the trying times—those dark and rainy days—if we are to ever enjoy the bounty that awaits us on the other side of the rainbow.

Day of the Dream

In the hot and hazy summer steam
I was carried off in a waking dream
Flipping through thoughts I've mused in the past
The tragic, the comic, the roles for the cast

Searching and striving to find the right way
Reaching and seeking, I dreamed of the day
I dreamed of starring in the greatest show
That would play on forever—what did I know?

The dream it fell like freezing rain
With a sharp and icy, chilling pain
But melted away as I kindled my fire
The flames and the curtain rose higher and higher

I opened my eyes late this afternoon
As a breeze sang softly a long-lost tune
I came to my feet and took a long bow
The day of the dream has always been now

While my brother John was out seeking fame and fortune on Broadway, I was out on a vision quest of my own, although not quite as ambitious as the one that he chose. As a young wanderlust in my early twenties, I set out on the open road on a soul-searching, cross-country journey. I treated myself to a smorgasbord of mountains, prairies, deserts, canyons, lakes, streams, oceans all complete with breath-taking sunrises and sunsets. The journey didn't do much for advancing me along a career path, but I have no regrets about how I spent that time of my life. It provided me with invaluable inspiration and appreciation for the wonderful land I am very proud to call home. When I look back on it now, it is a reminder to me that each and every moment of life is meaningful and extraordinary.

Mobile Magic

Been on the road five long days
Road-shocked, hot and gritty
Stirring up the desert sands
And blasting through the cities
Got a beat-up buggy
But I drive it with real style
Cruising through the country
Gets me higher every mile

If your feet begin to itch now,
Don't react too slow
Throw your idle dreams in gear
Then pack your bags and go
There's a certain mobile magic
I know you're bound to feel
When your spirit and the highway
Meet behind the wheel

Windshield is a painting
Of a creeping twilight sky
As the mirror shows a sunset
To the corner of my eye
Got no clock or map to go by
Always find my way
I'll keep on truckin' down the road
Until my dying day

*"Two roads diverged in a wood, and I took the one less
traveled by,
And that has made all the difference."*

~ Robert Frost

CHAPTER TWO
THE PHILOSOPHICAL FOUNDATIONS

Now, back to that aversion to naming and labeling I mentioned earlier—let me elaborate on that quirk of mine. I guess you can say that also goes back to my late teen years while attending college in upstate New York, but just a little bit of background first to set the stage.

Although I have been living in Georgia for more than twenty years now, I grew up on Long Island. My home town was not quite as rough as some areas of Long Island, like parts of Brooklyn or Queens for instance, but you still had to have a bit of tough skin to get along in the neighborhood where I grew up. As a young boy, I was basically a very peaceful and timid fellow, but life takes its toll and can rob us of our childhood innocence—at least to some degree. I grew up in the pleasant little suburban village of Baldwin on the south shore of "the island," as most people from Long Island and the surrounding areas of New York refer to it. My family and I lived in a middle-class neighborhood on the south side of town, which was predominantly Jewish. As a result, I went through grammar school with the erroneous impression that there were a lot more Jews in the world than there really were. It wasn't until later that I came to the realization that Jews make up only a small percentage of the world's population. There were only a handful of us Catholic kids who would get up and leave the grammar school on Wednesday afternoons to catch the bus to Catechism, while all the Jewish kids waited and looked on at the few of us "different" kids filing out the door. "There go the *goyim*," they might have been thinking to themselves. I was taught that Hebrew term for a "non-Jew" by my best friend who was, of course, a Jew himself.

You may be thinking to yourself, "Gee, how tough could it have been growing up in a middle class, Jewish neighborhood on Long Island?!" Well, you might be surprised to learn just how tough the Jews can be if you're foolish enough to cross them. The Israeli nation has been constantly attacked and involved in some sort of conflict the vast majority of time it has been in existence. Their warriors are extremely fierce and tenacious and, after enduring the Holocaust, you better believe the Israelis, as well as Jews living *anywhere* in the world, don't feel inclined to take crap from anybody. In fact, the biggest and toughest kid I could remember growing up was a very devout Jew who his friends affectionately referred to as "Bruce the Moose." Then there was my old buddy Alan Wasserman, also known as "Wasso." For the most part, he had a friendly and sort of hippie-like demeanor and enjoyed listening to the Beatles and Jimi Hendrix as much as anyone did in the late sixties. He wore paisley shirts, bell-bottom jeans, and liked to ride his Schwinn bicycle. He liked to build model cars and planes as a hobby. Sounds mellow enough, but the problem was if you made the mistake of crossing him, you would pay the price! If you dared to make it physical, he would light you up and take you out in a heartbeat! I saw him in action, and, believe me, it wasn't pretty.

Don't get me wrong. I don't mean to make it sound like all the Jews I grew up around were a big bunch of thugs and bullies. With a few exceptions, I never really saw them as much of a threat at all when it came to *starting* fights, but, if provoked; they sure could and would *finish* them. Despite the minor intimidation I occasionally experienced from the Jews in public schools—mostly because I was in a clear minority—the real pressure I felt from bullying was in the courtyard outside that Catholic parochial school I had to attend on Wednesday afternoons, and later in junior high school on Saturday mornings. It was there that I ran into the true bullies—tough Italian and Irish kids mostly—who just *had* to pick a fight almost every darn week. Peaceful as I was, I still didn't care to get my butt kicked so I was forced to toughen up a bit. Life takes its toll—innocence fades.

I took my first boxing lesson when I was eight years old at a sleep-away camp called Camp Acadia in Livingston Manor, New York, which was run by Our Lady of Lourdes Catholic Church based in New York City. Later on, during junior high school, I joined the wrestling team and also played some soccer to keep me on my toes around those hooligans at the junior high school. Then I sort of became one of them myself. In the seventh grade, I reunited with an old buddy, Paul Broder, from early childhood—that's right, one of those tough Jews—who got the boot from public school for causing too much trouble. He was allowed back to the public junior high school after "doing his time" at a private grammar school. We hung out constantly, roaming the neighborhood with lit sticks of incense dangling from our lips. Those sticks were appropriately called "punks," which was perfect because that's what we were, too. We would cruise around on mini bikes and get into all sorts of trouble and, yes, fights. We then took our show to the ice hockey rink, where you could get into fights just about all you wanted, and the only punishment was to do five minutes in the penalty box— awesome! We are still the closest of friends, and he will occasionally refer to me in a joking manner as a "dumb goy"— short for goyim—but only if provoked.

Mom visiting me at Camp Acadia. Livingston Manor, New York, 1969

After surviving the high school years, I entered my freshman year in college where I met my dear friend Robert (Bob) Vetter. I had attended the same high school as Bob, so I recognized his face when I saw him roaming the halls of our dormitory, Hulbert Hall—or as the students called it, "Phippie"—at the State University of New York at Oneonta. I introduced myself to Bob, and we quickly became very good friends and, just like Broder, we still are today. Bob is now an anthropologist and has very advanced knowledge in many cultures, but particularly Native American Indian culture. He also has another skill that many who come in contact with him may not realize. He is a highly accomplished martial artist who, by the time I met him at seventeen years old, was already so advanced that I knew enough not to dare mess with him, even with all the experience I had with physical altercations growing up. However, I was very intrigued by what he had to share in the broad area of martial arts and *especially* all the rich philosophy behind it.

Bob introduced me to a martial arts instructor he had been working out with at the college who was known around campus as Bujinin. Like Bob, he was also very well-versed in many different forms and styles of martial arts, but advocated an approach to the martial arts that was developed by the extraordinary martial artist Bruce Lee. The basic premise of this approach to the martial arts was to become familiar with as many different techniques from as many different styles and forms of martial arts as you can, while not *conforming* to any of them. He advocated that individuals should just take what is useful and works best for themselves, and discard the rest, thereby developing their own, unique form of artistic expression in the martial arts. Bruce Lee even struggled with calling this approach to the martial arts Jeet Kune Do because of the problems associated with naming and labeling. Bruce Lee believed that people, in general, tend to conform and cling to chosen patterns and beliefs to give themselves a sense of security. In fact, he advocated throwing away all ideals, patterns, and styles because they are limiting. He challenged people to look at a situation without naming it because he believed that naming it causes fear. What Bruce Lee advocated—and a path I chose to follow enthusiastically—was a philosophy that is not just limited to the martial arts, but one that could be applied to a wide variety of situations in life itself:

"Using no Way as Way – Having no Limitations as Limitations"

I made mention about the philosophy behind the martial arts, but there is also some religion involved as well. The symbol above, which is the symbol of Jeet Kune Do, contains the familiar yin-yang symbol within it. The yin-yang symbol originated from the ancient Chinese religion of Taoism, which drew some of its fundamental notions from the School of Yin-yang, and the teachings of Lao Tzu and Zhuangzi. The word "Tao" means "way" or "path." Volumes have been written about Taoism, so I'll try to keep it simple. In fact, simplicity is one of the basic tenets of Taoism, so that would be very appropriate. Other basic principles of Taoism include spontaneity, naturalness, and wu-wei. Wu-wei basically means action through non-action. For instance, sometimes the loudest messages can be delivered through sheer silence. All of us husbands can surely understand that concept when our wives are angry with us, and we get the silent treatment. Taoism also emphasizes the Three Treasures: humility, compassion, and moderation.

In the concept of yin-yang, yin represents darkness, female, negative, and cold, while yang represents light, male, positive, and heat. In Western culture, these two groupings are looked at as complete opposites, while in Taoism and other Eastern belief systems, they are viewed as complementary forces that work together in constant motion. The two arrows on the symbol above represent this constant motion. Also, notice that the yin contains a small spot of yang, and vice versa. This means that whenever something goes to an extreme—moderation is exceeded—the opposite or complementary force is bound to set in.

Here's a very simple example of this concept in action. As the sun rises in the morning, the darkness fades away and the sun heats the atmosphere. Gradually the day fades to night, the atmosphere cools, and it gets dark. If you think about it, sunrise and sunset occur constantly, and simultaneously, somewhere in the world at every moment of every day—constant motion. Another application of the concept of yin-yang, and one that really hits home with me, is the interaction of good and evil. Without evil, how would we even understand what good is? There would be nothing to which to compare it. I mentioned earlier how life takes its toll and can rob us of our childhood innocence—if we let it. In fact, sometimes, just in order to survive, any good person may occasionally need to be a little bit "bad-ass" to get by in this world. A balance must be struck.

"I never did sell my soul to the devil, but I guess you can say I let him rent for a while."

Many life experiences have made me feel as if I needed to make a "deal with the devil" for the sake of the greater good. I'm sure we've all felt like that at some time or another in our lives, especially if the outcome of the "evil deed" will be to the overall benefit of a loved one or to our families. The following poem, "Dark Star," was inspired by and written about one of my favorite rock stars. Jim Morrison certainly had his demons, and most definitely had a dark side, but he was also an inspired poet and love child of the sixties. He was living proof that good and evil can work together in yin-yang fashion to create magic in the world. Shine on Dark Star!

Dark Star

Dark Star shines upon us all
On good and bad its shadow falls
Air and Fire – Earth and Rain
Nothing else does stay the same

Scrap your life, trash the halls
Graffiti new on virgin walls
Lizard slithers out of skin
Thin the wall he hides within

Breaking through the eggshell clean
A beam of darkness shining mean
Hell and Heaven mesh together
Dark star will shine on forever

I suppose that last poem makes for a pretty good segue into the next branch of philosophical thought that also had a profound influence on my perspective on life. In William Blake's 1793 poem, "The Marriage of Heaven and Hell," he writes, "If the doors of perception were cleansed every thing would appear to man as it is, Infinite." This line inspired the great author, poet, and philosopher Aldous Huxley to write his short book *The Doors of Perception* where he described his experiences with the psychedelic drug mescaline. Jim Morrison was a fan of Aldous Huxley and his writings and was inspired to name his rock band the *Doors* in tribute to the famous Blake line that was immortalized by the Aldous Huxley book. As discussed in the Introduction, Huxley also wrote many other books, including *Brave New World*, which is one of my all-time favorites.

The notion of cleansing the doors of perception is closely akin to the philosophy of existentialism. It's time for another rewind to freshman year at SUNY Oneonta when I met a philosophy professor who would also have a great impact on my perception of the whole universe. I needed to take an elective and had heard about an interesting professor from India, Dr. Ashok Malhotra, who taught entry level philosophy. I signed up for his class, not really knowing what to expect, but it quickly became one of the most intriguing scholastic activities in which I had ever engaged. I recall Dr. Malhotra explaining early in the course how "philosophy poses many questions, but offers no answers." My first impression was that the course could end up being very frustrating—how would we be graded if there were no right or wrong answers?! But, like any good philosophy teacher, he knew the best way to help his students was not to tell them what they should or shouldn't think, but to teach them how to think for themselves. Point a finger in a direction and help them to find their own path. There is an old expression, credited to Taoism founder Lao Tzu, which goes, *"Give a man a fish and you feed him for a day. Teach a man to fish and you feed him for a lifetime."* In a sense, Dr. Malhotra taught me how to fish. All he ever fed me was food for thought.

Dr. Malhotra was a fan of the existentialist philosopher Jean Paul Sartre, and authored a book about two of Sartre's works—*Nausea* and *Being and Nothingness*. Like Taoism, volumes have been written about the topic of existentialism, so I'll try to do justice to Dr. Malhotra's simple approach to effectively teaching philosophy and hit upon just the basic concepts.

The basic tenet of existentialism is that people are completely free and are therefore responsible for what they make of themselves in their lifetime. In other words, we start life with a completely clean slate and then get to draw on it whatever we choose. We also have free will as we move along our life path and so have the ability to change our direction at any time. But to fully understand the ramifications of this philosophy, there must be some explanation and understanding of the concept of mysticism or mystical awareness. As Dr. Malhotra explained to us, there are many misconceptions about mysticism in Western culture just because of the word itself. It is sometimes confused with the word "mysterious" and thought to be some sort of enigmatic notion or surreptitious state of mind that could only ever be attained by some highly advanced guru or monk living high on a mountain top in Tibet. It is also confused with the terms "misty" or "foggy," which are absolutely not synonymous with mysticism. In fact, mysticism is the complete opposite. Reality could not be perceived any more sharply and clearly than when in a state of mystical awareness. It is the state of awareness when those doors of perception are truly cleansed.

Dr. Malhotra explained that there are three general levels of thought, which he illustrated by drawing a triangle that was divided into three levels. The base section of the triangle represents all our subconscious thoughts; those thoughts that drift through our head constantly throughout the day, and also, when we sleep. The middle section of the triangle represents conscious thought; those thoughts that guide us through all the deliberate actions and decisions that we consciously ponder on a daily basis. The top level of the triangle represents religious thought, where we tend to cogitate at a higher level about concepts beyond the mundane, such as peace, love, compassion, forgiveness, humility, brotherhood, and all the other virtues generally taught and emphasized in houses of worship. Then, at the very apex of the triangle, is mystical awareness. This is where it all comes together.

Dr. Malhotra explained that there are different rose-colored "glasses" though which we look at the world. Those glasses, he said, represent all our beliefs, cultural influences, past experiences, societal values, political inclinations, fears, and religious convictions, to name a few. These are all things that we learn over time; those things we tend to label, which give us a sense of comfort and security in our existence. A few examples of such labels are words such as Democrat, Republican, conservative, liberal, African-American, immigrant, Christian, Muslim, and so forth. Take a moment to reflect upon how your devotion to these or any other labels, structures and biases the way you view the world and others around you. These labels and all that come with them may also be viewed as those "doors of perception" referred to earlier. Once those tinted glasses are removed, this will allow us to experience reality in the purest, clearest, simplest, and most unadulterated way possible. Only then can we see clearly and truly understand and experience—in the present—the totality of existence. This is the state of mystical awareness; the clean slate that we started with, but with life experience behind it.

Hopefully, I explained that in simple enough terms to convey the basic concept, but the attainment of mystical awareness is certainly a lot easier said than done, as I'm sure you could imagine. Speaking of "imagine," John Lennon's "Imagine" ponders the concept of no religion in the world. In my opinion, the biases that people develop because of the religious beliefs ingrained in them as children or to which they committed as adults are the prejudices that are hardest to escape. Historically, religion creates the most passion in people, and therefore represents the darkest of those "tinted lenses" through which people view the world. I would say that nationalism—a strong sense of pride in a person's home country and allegiance to its customs and traditions—scores a very close second. All those things that are pounded into our psyche from such a young age, and ingrained in the very fabric of our being, are not so easy to shake loose, especially when strong emotions, such as love and fear, come into play. It takes a very open heart and mind to even begin to take that journey to the center of the soul, which is the pinnacle of the triangle. It sounds overwhelming and totally impossible, but it really isn't.

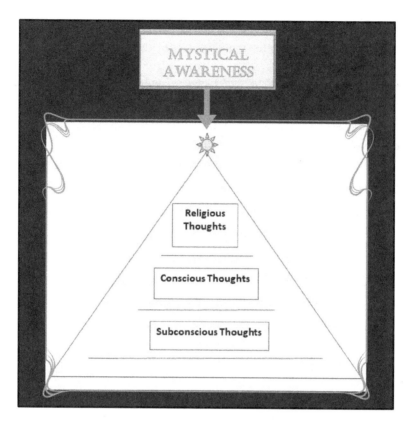

In my studies of Jeet Kune Do (JKD), I was taught how the truth is revealed through a similar process of shedding, rather than collecting and storing more and more knowledge. The latter practice will only clutter our minds further. An analogy was once presented to me that described how a sculptor carefully removes unnecessary pieces of rock from a slab of stone, one-by-one, until finally the desired image is revealed. In a similar fashion, we must try to chip away at all our preconceived notions and beliefs at least long enough to allow ourselves to comprehend what other schools of thought or religions have to offer. Then we will "get the picture." No need to abandon those beliefs altogether, and that's certainly not what I'm advocating, but you will never truly be able to interact with all others peacefully and harmoniously until you at least suspend your beliefs and attempt to put yourself in their place and try to see things from their perspective. You may come to the realization that you have more in common than you initially thought; there are many common denominators across different schools of thought.

My JKD instructor, Bujinin, had shared a story about a master martial artist who visited with a master of another style to compare notes. As the host master tried to explain to the other master about his style, he was constantly interrupted with comments like, "Yes that sounds a lot like what we do," and, "Oh yes, we have that too." Finally, the host master stopped talking and poured his guest a cup of tea. When the cup was full, he kept pouring the tea into the cup, and it began to spill over onto the table and the floor. The visiting master proclaimed, "What are you doing—no more can go into that cup!" His host replied, "Yes, that is true, but if you don't first empty your cup, how can you taste my cup of tea?" The moral of the story: the usefulness of the cup is in its emptiness. Buddhists refer to this state of absolute stillness and emptiness of the mind as *Shunyata*. It is a state of non-duality, which is also at the root of the ancient Hawaiian art of *Ho'oponopono*. No matter what the formal belief system, or what it is labeled, the point is that you will never be able to see things clearly when your mind is constantly prejudging every situation and is all cluttered up with all sorts of presuppositions. To be a *truly* good listener we must learn to let go, or things can get messy as with the spilt tea.

The following poem was inspired by all my wonderful teachers who helped me to broaden my horizons by urging me to be open-minded, and to stop worrying about what others may think of me should I dare to stray from the conformity in which I was raised.

The Soul Streaker

His feet were sore and tired, the pain he had to lose
So he loosened up the laces and kicked off both his shoes
Feeling rather smothered too; a stifled ragamuffin
He lost the tight and choking tie and opened his top button

His eyes were red and itchy, his tears thick as molasses
Splashed some water in his face and shed the dark sunglasses
He sweat just like a snitch in jail and so the story goes
He twitched and tossed and turned a bit then tore off all his
clothes

And there he stood stark naked; how bare a soul was he
Pure and bright and simple—immaculate and free

His shoes were those of culture that led him down a path
Conform to all their values or feel the neighbors' wrath
The tie it came from schooldays when they strangled out the boy
They filled his head with this and that and played him like a toy

The sunglasses were placed on him by preachers, nuns and priests
Believe in all we teach you son or answer to the beast
His clothes came from society; the politics of life
The job, the house, the car he drives, his perfect trophy wife

He travels with less baggage now; he's lost a heavy load
Running with more confidence along a smoother road
Dressed in just his pride and bliss and true serenity
The courageous old soul streaker goes dashing wild and free

"If you are always trying to be normal, you will never know how amazing you can be."

~ Maya Angelou

Aside from the great teachers and instructors we come upon in the classroom, there are also many lessons to learn from all those around us in life, including children or even child-like adults. We can all learn from the sage and the fool alike, but learning doesn't necessarily always take place in a formal and serious setting. Having a sense of levity and the ability not to take things too seriously can be conducive to learning and is virtuous. As stated by the great Irish writer and poet, Oscar Wilde, *"Life is much too important a thing ever to talk seriously about."*

One of my fellow students in college, John, took his philosophy and psychology studies to heart. He liked to drone on and on to his friends and classmates about very deep philosophical teachings and explain how Eastern philosophical thought can be reconciled with Western physics and psychology so that a universal world view can be formulated, blah-blah-blah. Don't get me wrong—I'm not knocking such insightful world-view philosophies. In fact, I embrace them myself, but I also try to be careful not to over-intellectualize about such matters. Less is more; plentitude is confusion, as the late Bujinin preached.

One day, as John went on and on about such acumens, his friend Greg—who was a bit of a jokester, to put it mildly— interrupted John and irreverently suggested, "Hey John, I got an idea. Why don't you just cut the Dharma crap and universal consciousness bullshit and just get a *grip* on life?" He clenched his hand into a fist to emphasize the word "grip." There was dead silence. I wrote the following poem to commemorate Greg's simple-minded brilliance:

Grasp the Art

Still the mind is playing games
Pills to stretch and tease the brain
Making love is still the same—
With yourself, then down the drain

Love and Anger bleed the knife
Desperados need a wife
Sophistication beckons strife
Grasp the art of living life!

Still those toss and turning nights
Strung out from the fear of fright
Hoping things will turn out right
But all the while losing sight

Art and science breed a man
Sketch your life then paint the plan
The image came when colors ran
Grasp the art, you'll understand

Although I am grateful for all those wise and insightful people—sages and fools alike—that I have had the privilege of learning from in the past, as suggested in "Grasp the Art," sophistication can lead to a life of strife. Sometimes our minds can become so cluttered with so much information and influence from others that we start losing touch with reality, and more importantly, with ourselves. Perhaps you may have even caught yourself, more than once, saying, "I don't know what came over me, I just wasn't myself." Sometimes we might try too hard to play a role or portray an image that we feel is expected of us. In the process of trying to meet what we perceive to be the expectations of others, we can lose sight of who we *truly* are. This notion of role-playing brings to mind a quote by Raymond Hull, coauthor of the book *The Peter Principle*, who said, *"He who trims himself to suit everybody soon whittles himself away."*

Follow Your Heart

I know what I want and I'm right on the brink
But oh, so hung up on what they will think
Pacing and musing on which way to go
It's all so confusing—I just don't know

Make up your mind to make a new start
You'll set yourself free if you follow your heart

I don't want to stifle, I don't want to hide
They're more than a trifle, these feelings inside
I'm oh, so uptight, it's just so unreal
It could all be so right if I'd show what I feel

Wake up today and make that new start
The only true way is to follow your heart

"Far better to live your own path imperfectly than to live another's perfectly."

~ Bahavagad Gita

It's during times when we question who we really are that we need to turn our thoughts deeply inward and just *remember*. Some people don't actually believe that there is a soul or spirit in and around our physical bodies, but I suspect that most people do. As for myself, I believe that I *am* a soul who just happened to have acquired a body somewhere along the way. That once untainted and innocent soul also happened to pick up a lot of baggage along the way since acquiring that body. Am I a lover or am I a fighter? Am I an intellectual or a merry prankster? Maybe

I'm all of the above? After struggling with an identity crisis for many years like most "normal" young people do growing up, I finally decided that *I* am my own best friend and the only one who I can *really* trust. He's the old soul streaker who I turn to when I really need some good advice—the deeply reflective man in the mirror. The answers to our most important questions in life lie deep within us.

"Meditate. Live purely. Be quiet. Do your work with mastery. Like the moon, come out from behind the clouds! Shine."

~ Buddha

Journey to the Center of the Soul

This morning when I woke up
I wondered what would be
A hundred million questions
Now are plaguing me
Yet here I sit contented
Because in time I've learned
It never pays to worry
Just to be concerned

Sometimes I need some friendship
Sometimes it's seldom felt
But never am I less alone
Than when I'm by myself

I'd like to tell this story
But I don't know where to start
So I won't try in vain to say it
But I'll show it with my heart
Sun comes up, sun goes down
Time slips by, world goes 'round
What you're really meant to do
Comes before your time is through

Sometimes I need some loving
Sometimes I need some help
But never am I less alone
Than when I'm by myself

"Your inner voice is the voice of divinity. To hear it, we need to be in solitude, even in crowded places."

~ A.R. Rahman

CHAPTER THREE
LOSING MY RELIGION

Many people may recognize the title of this chapter as the title of a popular song by the alternative rock band from Georgia, R.E.M. That is true, but the phrase "losing my religion" is an expression that comes from the southern region of the United States that refers to when someone is "at the end of his rope" and loses his temper. If you listen to the lyrics to the R.E.M. song, you may also pick up on the theme of unrequited love—when you pour your heart and soul into something, or someone, but just don't feel any reciprocation.

I mentioned earlier that I believe that religion is perhaps the one aspect of humanity that holds the tightest grip on the masses, and the one that people are most passionate about. Strictly from my own observances, I find that people are less likely to be open to other belief systems the more devout they are in their own religious beliefs. I don't know that anyone ever took a survey, but I also suppose that most of those pious and devoted followers had their religious beliefs ingrained in them from a very young age, like they were for me. Being raised in a Roman Catholic household, I was baptized before I even had an inkling of what religion was. As a young boy, I had received my First Holy Communion and then it was just about a hop, kneel, and a prayer to my Confirmation as a "bona fide" member of the Catholic

Church when I was still a young teenager.

Although I experienced some hard times with tough bullies and strict nuns—sometimes a fine line between the two—while attending those catechism classes I had to attend, my experiences with the church were not all bad. I particularly got drawn in around the holidays when people are caught up in the giving spirit of the season. To this day, I still look forward to Christmastime because people just seem more inclined to be kind to each other, to help others, and to do other good deeds. Of course, not everyone is like that, but the negativity of all the dreary curmudgeons tends to be suppressed by the group consciousness of the good around Christmastime. I believe there is a synergistic effect to that whole "pay-it-forward" mentality. It is a mindset that helps society to transcend to a higher level—a level where people can feel good about themselves and each other. It is when people rise up from that mundane center section of the triangle to the more virtuous upper section. This poem was inspired by that time of year when all the air is lit by the magic of brotherhood and is dedicated to the one that it is all about—believe in Him or not.

Christmas Time

Dim the lights and kindle the fire
The snow is cold, wind is dire
Distant voices sing a rhyme
The ancient tale of Christmastime

Windows glow with candle light
Nothing can go wrong tonight
Across the sky a shooting star
Delivers spirit from afar

On the wings of soaring dove
Messages of endless Love
Everything is crystal clear
Our Savior Christ the Lord is here!

I wish that the wondrous display of human nature that occurs at Christmastime would perpetuate throughout the year, but yang eventually fades to yin. I opened my heart and soul to my religion, like I was taught, as did my four siblings. I guess you can say there is much truth to the old adage that "ignorance is bliss." According to my interpretation of Genesis in the *Bible*, that's why things went south for Adam and Eve; they just had to go and eat from that tree of knowledge. But isn't that what we all do? I don't ever remember school being optional. We learned about such "wonderful" things such as the Crusades when, according to which version of history we read, the Catholics attacked the followers of Islam for centuries for believing in their different Abrahamic god Allah and, especially after the death of the prophet Mohammed, for aggressively trying to spread their Islamic beliefs. We also learned about how the Italian philosopher Giordano Bruno was condemned as a heretic and both tortured and persecuted—burned at the stake—by the Roman Inquisition for persistently defending his controversial theories on cosmology and the universe. Not to mention, we also learned in science classes at school how the earth was formed when cosmic dust came together to form solid masses that collided and brought with them the building blocks of life.

One night as I caught a ride home from a concert and was stuck in traffic with a good friend of mine, we somehow got into a discussion about astronomy, and I marveled at how amazing it is that we are all related to each other through the cosmos, and how the basic elements of which we are all composed come from the same cosmic dust of the stars. I was immediately taken back when she quickly retorted, "We didn't come from no stardust. We came from Adam and Eve. That's what *I* believe!" Uh-oh! "Darn it," I thought to myself, "I need to remember that I'm living in the *Bible* belt now." After an awkward silence that seemed to last for an eternity, I finally asked, "So, how about that Journey concert?"

After this experience, I did some thinking about the whole debate over creation versus evolution and decided to research *exactly* what the "Good Book" says about the creation of man. This is what I found:

Genesis 2:7 - "*And the Lord God formed man of the dust of the ground, and breathed into his nostrils the breath of life; and man became a living soul.*"

Wait a minute, back up just a second. What's that word I see that describes what God formed man out of? Do I see the word "dust?" Hmmm, what do you know. We did come from dust after all? At least it says so right there in the *Holy Bible*. Maybe that's part of the reason why so many of the scientists who believe in evolution are also very religious? This may seem like an outrageous question to both hard-core creationists and evolutionists, but is there a common thread here? Perhaps it was the process of evolution that was created by the intelligent design of a supreme force or being; not the work of some wizard-like God who waved his magic wand and conjured up two adult human beings? These questions are food for thought, but the stricter an interpretation one has of the *Bible* or of the teachings of Darwinism or Friedrich Nietzsche, the harder it is to be receptive of such assertions. Another way of putting it is that once individuals take sides and *label* themselves as either an evolutionist or creationist, they may not be so likely to drop their stance long enough to even consider how the two schools of thought could possibly be even vaguely akin and ultimately be reconciled. "Not my cup of tea," they each are thinking, or something a lot worse.

I am keenly aware that by even raising such questions I may be considered a heretic by some, including fundamentalists in the Catholic Church, but then again Giordano Bruno was considered a heretic back in his time also. It turns out that the sun *is* the center of our solar system, and the earth *is* spherical. So, you can go ahead and label me a heretic if you like, but keep in mind that the only way that Christianity has survived more than 2000 years is because of its ability to adapt to changing times and circumstances, much like the way different, morphing species have survived the millennia as their environments changed. I suppose that is something that the two chameleons—Christianity and evolution—have in common? Maybe one day people will not be considered heretics for questioning if God perhaps created man (indirectly) *through* the intelligent design of evolution. Maybe that will even be the official interpretation of Genesis 2:7 by most churches sometime out in the future, but for now, I'm not completely feeling the love. However, the following quote by Pope Francis gives me a great deal of hope:

"Evolution in nature is not inconsistent with the notion of creation, because evolution requires the creation of beings that evolve."

~ Pope Francis

As you might have deducted from what I described earlier about my childhood and teen years, I definitely gravitated toward the macho persona, especially as I advanced through the ranks in both hockey and martial arts. Although I *am* essentially a typical American male, I was still slightly out of balance, leaning toward the masculine "yang" in all aspects of my personality in addition to just the physical aspects. That being the case, I was often very outspoken about homosexuality. I was good for all the ignorant, stereotypical clichés such as, "they are freaks of nature" or "I can't think of anything more sick and disgusting than what they do to each other." I eventually came to deeply regret ever uttering such ignorant and insensitive banalities, and especially for articulating them in the presence of my siblings.

Growing up in a house with six other people, I was made to share a bedroom with my younger brother John. We got along pretty good, for the most part, and played a lot of chess matches against each other in that bedroom. However, being the oldest of four boys, and having that macho persona, I was the "older brother nightmare." I would pick on all of them to some degree, but John definitely got the worst of it. I would sit on his chest and hang drool down in his face and suck it back up before it got to him—well, most of the time—and likewise "torture" him in a variety of other juvenile ways. John was always a bit more sensitive than my other brothers, though, and reacted very strongly when I picked on him. Sometimes I thought he really *over*-reacted. Whatever the case, I earned my dad's size thirteen shoe planted on my rump on more than one occasion because John shrieked like I was murdering him when he might have only been the victim of some relatively minor verbal intimidation.

I mentioned earlier that John eventually came to be a very successful Broadway actor. John was only about eighteen or nineteen years old when he landed a major role as "Bobby" in the leviathan Broadway play, *A Chorus Line*. It was about that time that he came to me and wanted to talk about something.

I can imagine how difficult I must have made it for him to look me in the eye and bravely tell me that he was gay. By that time, I had already assumed that he was gay because of observable characteristics, so I quickly let him know in the kindest and most understanding way I could that I had already figured it out. I wanted to spare further discomfort for both of us. I also reassured him that our conversation changed nothing, and that he was my brother who I would always love no matter what. However, still being very naïve and ignorant about homosexuality, I did have to ask him if he felt like he was pressured into that lifestyle, so he could succeed in his chosen profession. He didn't flinch, and his immediate comeback was that as far back as he could think into his earliest childhood memories; he had always had those sorts of feelings where he was attracted to males and not the opposite sex. It was then that it truly sank in for me that there really is no choice involved in the matter of homosexuality for gay people. It is simply a component of their very constitution; they are born that way.

Fortunately, it was easy enough for me to understand and accept my brother's situation, but what about others in society who may not have that same *family* love for a person who is gay? What about the Roman Catholic Church that we were raised in? Houston, we have a problem.

As the years went by, I could see John's cynicism for the church grow, and the caustic affect it had on him to know that the church he was baptized and confirmed in did not accept him for who he was. Even worse, they suggested his sexual orientation was not because of the way God created him, but rather a manifestation of some sort of evil or demons within. It was especially sad because I remember John loving the season of Christmas more than any of us five kids living in the house. The bitterness he displayed hit home with me, and hurt me also. I often thought, "What kind of a religion puts you in a situation where you have to take sides with either the church or your own brother?" This is especially hard to digest once you understand that there is absolutely no choice in the matter other than the decision to hide one's sexual orientation, thereby living a lie— another sin. Essentially, this was a no-win situation, and my brother was effectively banished from the church he grew up worshipping in. Ever since ancient times, many belief systems have considered banishment to be one of the worst kinds of punishment. So, you have to ask, "Does the sentence really fit the 'crime' of homosexuality?"

Then things got even more personal. When I was about twenty-four years old, I met the woman who I would eventually marry and together raise three wonderful children. Being a baptized and confirmed Catholic, it never crossed my mind that I would ever do something that would cause me to be prohibited from receiving the sacrament of marriage in a Catholic Church. My fiancé, also a Catholic, had been through a divorce, so the deal was that I could still get married in a Catholic Church, but she couldn't. So once again, it came down to choosing between the church and who I loved.

Both incidents left me really wondering about, and definitely did not set well with my understanding of, some of the concepts that I was taught in church, such as forgiveness, righteousness, and non-judgement of others. I understand that forgiveness does not necessarily mean there will be no consequences for your actions, but what did I do? The message I got was that I decided to fall in love with the wrong person and so, had to pay the price for that, sort of like the situation with my brother and the hand that he was dealt. We are all human beings and therefore not perfect.

I once saw a post on a social media site that asserted Pope Francis had made comments to the effect that Adam and Eve were not real, and that gay people should be accepted into the church and be allowed to marry. It was followed by numerous other posts by people who were thrilled to hear this news and how wonderful it was that a new age was dawning, marked with hope for the future, and many other similar comments. Of course, my hoax radar went off right away, and I quickly figured out by doing a little research that it was all a bunch of hogwash. I really did feel badly, though, for all those people who believed the gibberish and were given false hope. I was struck by the number of people out there who are in support of a Pope making such declarations, if he were to make them, and that hardly *anyone* wrote bad things about it. Maybe some people just fear that something bad would happen to them if they spoke poorly of a Pope? Anyway, I did see a sincere glimmer of hope that the church may be evolving and addressing some of these issues. When I researched the above hoax, I discovered that Pope Francis had said, "*If someone is gay who searches for the Lord and has goodwill, who am I to judge?*" It's a start anyway.

We always hear about the virtues of religious tolerance and how we really need to be sensitive to all the other belief systems around the world in order for society, especially American society, to function at a higher level. What we may not hear as much about, however, is the need for us to sometimes tolerate our *own* religion, or religion in general. I'm sure you understand what I mean when you hear stories on the news about faithful, long-time parishioners being banned for not tithing, or members of clergy molesting young people who serve in the church. This next poem may seem very harsh and cynical, but my intent is not to condemn religion or turn people against it, but rather to emphasize some of the hypocrisy that exists in religion. However, criticizing or judging without showing any compassion or forgiveness would make me a hypocrite myself. My true hope and desire, therefore, is that all the religions of the world may continue to recognize mistakes made in the past and continue to evolve as they have for thousands of years. In other words, may they never be condemned to repeat history. My good friend Bob once told me he believed that, at their highest levels of interpretation, all religions mesh. There are many paths with many labels that lead to a state of enlightenment. Taoists will refer to this path as "The Tao" or "The Way," Native Americans may refer to it as "The Red Road," while Buddhists, Hindus, Christians, Shamans, and other religions and cultures all have their own paths with their own particular labels. Yet, all these paths up the mountain of truth all lead to the same summit, no matter what name or label is given to either the path or the summit. Those who transcend the limitations of strict religious dogma and reach that summit realize that we are all one and the labels become worthless.

Tolerate Religion

Genesis and procreation
Hear Ye now this Revelation
God is good, God is great
But cross him and beware your fate

Love thy neighbor and love thyself
Reject the devil, and sins of wealth
Forgive the villains all full of hate—
And toss some bucks in the offer plate
All are welcome, please come and pray
Oh, but wait—that one is gay!
Sing the hymns, what joyful noise
And please don't touch those altar boys

Pray for those who do you wrong
And steal from you life's sweet, sweet song
Do good deeds with no set ration
Salvation comes from true compassion

Pathetic, foolish human race
Our eyes have failed us—blind as Faith
How ironic that in the name of Religion
We've justified so much damn killing

The world is precious and life divine
So break some bread and drink some wine
Religion takes us just so far—
A distant, shining Guiding Star

Believe what you want, but no one knows
Exactly what eternity holds
For it is only in the end, you see,
That we'll learn the meaning of being free

Majestic, noble human race
Kings and Queens of time and space
Be humble; respect your brothers' views
Though you may sit in different pews

To be bitter, spiteful, vindictive, and all full of resentment is never a good way to deal with situations where we feel that someone or something has done wrong by us. No good can come from harboring such negative emotions and "losing our religion." However, we all know that it's usually only the loudest of voices of protest that receive any attention and bring about change. If people don't rise up with civility and at least voice their objections to the things they don't think are right, then it is unlikely that anything will ever be done about them. It is through our own apathy, complacency and, especially, the *fear* of what others may think of us for speaking our minds that certain problems perpetuate. Don't complain that things will never change if you are not willing to dare to be a catalyst to the changes that you seek or hope for.

I am grateful to live in a country where we can offer our opinions without the fear of the government dragging us off to jail and cutting our tongues out. I won't ever take the right of freedom of speech for granted, or many of our other freedoms for that matter. However, if you really want to be heard in an effective manner, it is all in the delivery. Sometimes actions—or actions through non-action, *wu-wei*—speak even louder than words. Dropping attendance levels in any particular church, for instance, ought to send out a loud and clear message that something may be wrong.

I mentioned earlier how difficult it may be to imagine a world without any religion. For some people, namely atheists, that is no problem whatsoever. From my own experiences with atheists, I can say for sure that I have noted a great deal of their contempt and disdain for religion as a whole. They generally look at it as an indelible blemish on the face of mankind that they will never forgive or forget. There particularly seems to be a great deal of bitterness amongst atheists over all the wars that have been fought and lives that have been lost over the centuries because of religious differences, the Crusades being a typical and classic example. "Thou shalt not kill," they preached, unless the sons-of-bitches don't pray to the same God as us! Then we'll bust a cap in their blasphemous heads! I know, I know. They fought with swords. It's just an expression. However, as we should all be painfully aware of, the religious-based killings still persist to this very day.

I understand the umbrage that atheists have for religion, but I still choose to believe that there *is* indeed a spiritual dimension to our existence. However, I'm not a firm believer that when we die we'll be greeted by either Saint Peter at the Pearly Gates of Heaven or by pitch fork-wielding demons cavorting about the gates of Hades. In the poem "Tolerate Religion," you might have noticed the line that goes, *"For it is only in the End, you see, that we'll learn the meaning of being free."* This may sound a bit agnostic, and maybe I am, although I detest those darn labels! I believe that some things you just don't know, and can't know, until you experience them for yourself. I have had the concept of "faith" drilled into my head from a very young age, but I also happen to personally know four different people who were clinically dead and came back to describe their experiences to me, and neither pearly gates nor fire and brimstone were mentioned by any of them. However, they all *did* have extraordinary experiences and remembered what they saw and felt. We'll see.

Good and Evil

Good and evil knit so tight
It's hard to tell what's wrong or right
Flex the soul with all your might
And chase the balance day and night

"Come make love," black widow said
Grinning through her veil of dread
Sweet, sweet ecstasy upon her bed
Claimed her seed, then left him dead

Good and Evil dance in time
God and Devil sing in rhyme
Here's an evil clue divine—
Both are vital friends of mine

"All human beings are commingled out of good and evil."

~ Robert Louis Stevenson

"The awful thing is that beauty is mysterious as well as terrible. God and devil are fighting there, and the battlefield is the heart of man."

~ Fyodor Dostoevsky

The atheists are certainly entitled to their opinions, and I have already expressed how I believe that it is not only our right, but also our duty and responsibility, to speak up and voice our sentiments. However, I have a major dispute with atheists who I've known. They are so fervent in their belief that spirit does not exist, they tend to refuse to recognize any evidence of the existence of spirit, or anything paranormal for that matter. That goes for both physical and metaphysical evidence alike. They tend to reject any proof gathered using cameras and other electronic devices as a bunch of crap, and also look at anyone who claims to be a medium as a total whack-job charlatan; no matter how spot-on they are with their visions of things that they could not possibly have learned about previously. At the same time, they put down the creationists who reject the science of evolution because creationists generally refuse to accept any of the scientific evidence that has been collected in support of evolution. So, I see a bit of stubbornness and hypocrisy in both religious extremism and atheism.

Since the study of death and what actually happens when we die is a relatively new field of study, my prediction for the future is that scientists will eventually find an empirical explanation for what is commonly referred to by the religious as "soul" and "spirit." I suspect that it might be described in general terms as a vibrational life-force energy that permeates and surrounds all living things, just as many people currently believe, but the particular properties, physics, and dynamics of that energy will be more clearly understood and defined in scientific terms. If, or dare I say *when,* this finally happens, I also suspect that both atheists and religious fundamentalists will go scrambling for ways to vehemently refute such evidence, or at least figure out ways to put their own spin on it. Right now, it seems like the bulk of any real strong proof, aside from that collected through controversial electronic devices, is primarily based upon the testimony of either people who were clinically dead and then regained consciousness, or from mediums and other "sensitives" who have demonstrated their extraordinary ability to pick up on details about those who have passed. Those poor mediums catch a lot of flak from both atheists and the deeply religious. While atheists dismiss them as phonies, the religious reject them as people who merely practice witchcraft, or do the work of the devil. It appears to me that people at both extremes have their filters on; they just see and hear what they want in regard to this very touchy subject of spirit and soul. It does make for some great food for thought though, and also provides inspiration to compose. Philosophy asks many questions but provides no answers. My prediction may not ever materialize, at least not in my lifetime, but I can hypothesize.

Another spark that ignites passion, and also something that fuels the fire of atheism, is when people interpret *Bible* verse in a way that supports their personal views and opinions, no matter how unreasonable those views and opinions may be. While on a business trip to Minneapolis, Minnesota, I once noticed a group of young black men dressed in robes and engaging in some street-corner preaching. As I walked past them, I picked up on their theme of exclusion. If you were not a descendant of one of the twelve tribes of the Israelites, or in other words a person of color, then the Lord God considered you to be no better than "spittle." "You are nothing," they shouted. This all according to Isaiah 40:17 and other verses they twisted and defiled to support their radical views. Then I heard something that made me stop dead in my tracks, do an about-face, and confront the false prophets. "Death to white people!" they all shouted with odious venom on their breath. According to the *Bible?* Really?!

I stood and listened to the nefarious haters as others, both white and black, gathered around and debated with them. Eventually, I decided to speak up myself and address the leader, who his faithful followers referred to simply as "the master."

"I've been listening to what you've been saying," I said, "and I've got to admit that I am probably not going to sleep tonight."

"He's not going to sleep tonight!" the one they called "master" rejoiced loudly, thinking that his message got through to me and that I had truly conceded that I was condemned to burn in hell because I am white. As they all reveled and celebrated their apparent victory, I spoke up again and said, "I am probably not going to sleep tonight because I have never felt so sorry for anyone in my whole life as I do for all of you right now." I then proceeded to tell each and every one of them that I loved them, because that is what religion has taught *me* to do. Instead of "losing my religion," I flashed them all the peace sign as I calmly strolled away smiling at them. Some glared back at me with disdain, but I caught a minute hint of shame on some of the other young dark faces who would not look me in the eye.

It crossed my mind that if the *Bible* could be used in such a way to spread hatred against white people, it wouldn't surprise me to find that there are probably other *Bible* verses that others have perverted to discriminate against people of color. Sure enough, after looking into this possibility I learned that slave owners had referenced the curse of Ham (son of Noah) and his descendants to sanctify and support their own interests in slavery. The depravity and distortion of Biblical verse doesn't end there.

Sometimes *Bible* verse is taken way too literally. I once read about a political candidate in Oklahoma named Scott Esk who indicated that if legislation were to be introduced that called for gay people to be stoned to death, he would support it. His reasoning was that stoning gays to death is supported by the *Old Testament*. Let's think about this for a second. The government stoning people to death in America in the 21st century because of their sexual orientation—does this <u>sound</u> like a good idea? The *Bible* also says that if a woman is not a virgin on her wedding night, then she should be stoned to death at the door of her father's house (see Deuteronomy 22:20-21). I understand the importance of having good moral fortitude, which is my own interpretation of the *spirit* of this verse, but would the enforcement of this prescribed punishment for having premarital sexual intercourse really be such a good idea either? It sounds a tad harsh and violent to me. In fact, anyone could research the topic of violence in the *Bible* and *Quran* and be a bit taken back by what you might find. For instance, I personally find it hard to justify that the following verse is the product of any *true* spiritual struggle:

Quran (8:12): *"I will cast terror into the hearts of those who disbelieve. Therefore strike off their heads and strike off every fingertip of them."*

Many people, especially in American society, talk about how violent the *Quran* is but while researching this topic I also discovered that there is an abundance of theological debate going on about which book actually contains more violence. It's sad but true, and so long as people continue to embrace verse like the one above as the true religious "law" that they must follow for all of eternity, achieving world peace will continue to be a very tough nut to crack. This example is not much different than the one above where *Bible* verse was given as a reason for eradicating whites, or the ones that were twisted to justify slavery and imply inferiority of gays, so I'm not just singling out fundamentalist Muslims and Islam.

"Anyone who knows God cannot be cruel. And anybody who engages in cruelty cannot know God. It is as simple as that!"

~ Sri Sri

"So in everything, do to others what you would have them do to you, for this sums up the Law and the Prophets."

~ Matthew 7:12 (NIV)

The point here is that anytime someone takes an extreme view or literal interpretation of religious dogma, it usually leads to very passionate conflict with those who don't share the same views. It's the same vicious cycle as with racial conflict. For instance, when claims are made by one religion that their God is the only *true* God, then how is that assertion *not* contentious or even insulting to people who believe in another God? They are basically saying that they are right and everyone else is wrong. But if you disagree with them, chances are that you will be the one accused of being insulting. Perhaps "God" is a divine and infinite living spirit that permeates everything in nature, as millions of pantheists believe, and not the monotheistic God, who created man in His own image, that either Christians or Muslims believe in? Are all of those masses of people dead wrong also?

So, am I saying that I think religion is simply bad? Of course, I'm not. Do I think that people who don't have any religion in their life are bad people? No, I'm certainly not saying that either. Do I think people sometimes take religious verse way too literally or place too much emphasis on religious and philosophical differences and trying to convert people over to their own beliefs as opposed to putting more effort into understanding all the similarities that exist between their own beliefs and those of others? Absolutely! **It is not religion itself that is corrupt; it is people—and certain people more than others—who have corrupted religion.** If you consider the notion that all religions interconnect at their highest levels of interpretation, and recall the analogy to how a sculptor reveals an image by removing unnecessary pieces of stone, it may start making sense. Once again, whole books have been written about the subject of religions coexisting peacefully, including *Oneness: Great Principles Shared by All Religions,* by Jeffrey Moses, which you may want to explore, or visit onenessonline.com. One of the principles referenced in the book that I was particularly drawn to is that we should follow the *spirit* of the scriptures, not the words.

"Study the words, no doubt, but look behind them to the thought they indicate; and having found it, throw the words away, as chaff when you have sifted out the grain."

~ Hinduism

Does this sound familiar? Take what is useful and discard the rest? If you chip away the unnecessary pieces of stone from that big ugly rock, a beautiful image can be revealed. Despite the fact that I obviously do not advocate beheading people, or stoning people to death with those discarded rock chips, you'll notice that I do quote religious scripture throughout this book. This is because I have found that there are many words of wisdom within those scriptures that are worth quoting, and also worth living by the spirit of, despite all those that don't particularly appeal to me. I often wondered when attending mass, just how many people are just mechanically repeating words of the scriptures—over and over—that they have memorized but have never really grasped the true spirit of, let alone committed to actually living by. I also believe it is possible that even those who are atheists can agree with, and live by, some of the principles explained in Jeffrey Moses's literary work, including the one about following the spirit of the scriptures referenced above. If they can only manage to put aside their caustic anger and resentment long enough to forgive the religious zealots who have harmfully distorted the meaning of religion over the ages, and brought fear and hatred into the emotional miasma of religious belief, perhaps they would be more inclined to see the wisdom behind some of those *Bible* verses, as well as words of wisdom from other religions as well.

In fact, the very act of forgiveness is a virtue stressed throughout the *Bible* and other religions of the world, and one that will truly set you free. It is really an amazingly powerful quality that many stubborn, bitter, and vindictive people may never learn and benefit from. After a tragic shooting in 2015 at the Emanuel African Methodist Episcopal (AME) Church in

Charleston, South Carolina, committed by a deranged white supremacist, some family members of the victims declared their forgiveness of the shooter, Dylan Roof, who murdered nine Christians in cold blood during a *Bible* study. Roof's desire was to see the violence escalate into a race war, but instead he was very graciously and effectively cut down to size by the magnificent power of forgiveness. In August 2015, just a few months after this incident, a group of white bikers of faith from Georgia contacted a group of black faith riders from the Atlanta area and organized a unified group that they called *Engines for Emanuel.* They arranged to ride in solidarity to the Emanuel AME in what they billed as a non-partisan and non-denominational event to show support, love, and unity. They all rode off together on a three-hundred-mile trek to visit the South Carolina church to attend service and deliver a check for fifteen thousand dollars that they raised from donations. Their actions should set an example for us all, religious or not.

"To err is human, to forgive, divine."

~ Alexander Pope

Forgiving is not the same as forgetting, and I can't emphasize enough how forgiving is something that we need to do for ourselves. Being a native New Yorker, I can't ever forget the attacks of September 11, 2001, on the World Trade Center in New York City and will always condemn them as one of the most despicable acts in the history of mankind. However, people who have been consumed by evil love nothing more than to know that they have stripped you of your enjoyment of life and brought you over to the dark side. The demons that support such attacks are just happily prancing about rejoicing in their lowly lairs, and growing ever stronger the more they feel the anger, resentment, and hatred welling up in your heart. They feed off that negativity and, so they get to bask in the glory of their loathsome attacks long after they are over. They took enough from us, so why capitulate and give them that long-term pleasure and satisfaction also? They don't deserve it, and we don't deserve to be *permanently* robbed of our happiness. That is not the proper way to honor those who lost their lives, nor would they want it that way. So, forgive, and trust that the universe will provide justice, but always remain vigilant—and never forget. This goes for any nation or group of people who have been wrongfully attacked, including attacks within our own borders.

In closing on this chapter, I would just like to express that I have grown terribly weary of hearing all the emotional debates between those who believe in creation versus those who believe in evolution, or those who believe in God (or spirit of any sort) and those who do not. In 1947, a chaplain named Peter Marshall said, "*...because if we don't stand for something, we shall fall for anything.*" Although I believe there is wisdom in those words, I once saw a woman wearing a tee shirt that said something I liked even better:

"If only people with closed minds also came with closed mouths"

CHAPTER FOUR
WE'RE NOT GUN A TAKE IT!

Love will light the path we pave—fear's the highway to our grave.

I was only ten years old through most of 1969, but I was still very aware that I was living in a time of social and political upheaval that was not even remotely like any of the decades that preceded the sixties. All you had to do was watch TV and see that traditional shows like *Howdy Doody, Captain Kangaroo,* and *The Lone Ranger* were fading away to the more zany, racy, and futuristic programs such as *The Monkees, Rowan and Martin's Laugh In,* and *Star Trek.* Instead of greasers and geeks, there were the mop-headed beatniks, followed by long-haired hippies all garbed in fringed leather vests, tie-dyed shirts, and bell-bottomed jeans with peace sign and flower patches all over them. Legions flocked to Woodstock for three days of peace, love, and music. There were those awesome psychedelic Peter Max posters printed in day-glow colors that lit up like magic under black lights. Lava lamps glowed with their mesmerizing dancing blobs undulating in a bedroom that vibrated with the spacy sounds of Jimi Hendrix and Jefferson Airplane blaring from huge speakers hooked to a turntable. Speaking of spacy, there was also the historic moonshot that left us with the timeless image of American astronauts saluting our flag on the surface of the moon, whether you believe that happened or not.

But the sixties weren't all fun and games. We also saw the rise of groups such as the Black Panthers and the Black Liberation Army protesting against decades of oppression and abuse. We saw the assassination of great leaders like President John F. Kennedy and the Rev. Dr. Martin Luther King. LSD-guzzling Timothy Leary urged people to "Turn on, tune in, drop out." Violence in the streets and on college campuses reached unprecedented levels as young people expressed their outrage at the war in Viet Nam by burning the American flag and their draft cards. The Viet Nam War—or "conflict" as it was called—was really at the center of the violently swirling vortex that *was* the sixties. It was the event that brought the element of fear to a young generation who was crying out for peace, love, and brotherhood of man. It was what snatched young, hairy teenagers out of their warm, comfortable worlds of psychedelic fantasy and left them bald, cold, and trembling with fear in the hostile rice paddies and jungles of Nam.

As I entered my teens during the early seventies, I had already witnessed several of my older sister's friends struggle with the fear of this nightmarish calamity as their draft cards showed up in the mail one-by-one. One friend of my sister's, Walter, did get sent over there. I remember him sitting in our family living room in Baldwin dressed in full uniform with a close buzz-cut and service cap lying on his lap, and politely trading military stories with my dad. I'm sure Dad shared some stories about his time stationed in Italy serving in the Army Fifth Infantry and tried to give Walter a good pep talk. Sadly, Walter retuned from his tour of duty early after being discharged with a severe mental disorder. That is a polite euphemism for stating that whatever the hell he experienced over there made him completely lose his marbles. I would look on in bewilderment at times when I noticed him vigorously pedaling around town on a bicycle with his eyes bulging wide open and his long hair flowing in the breeze. It was really hard for me to process that he was actually that same clean-cut uniformed soldier who I remembered sitting in our living room speaking with my dad. It was spectacles like this that left a big, ugly dent on my young and impressionable twelve-year-old mind in regard to war and being drafted.

I started to feel the walls closing in on me, and remember thinking, *"It's only a matter of time until it's my turn."* Call me a coward, but living life on the killing floor in the late sixties and early seventies did not appeal to my generally passive and diplomatic nature, especially after personally witnessing the aftermath of one of the war's victims and seeing and hearing many other horror stories daily in the news. Fights in the schoolyard or hockey rink were one thing, but this was real serious business. I knew my dad proudly served our country during World War II, but that really was a significantly different situation. The free world was united against our enemies, led by tenacious and diabolical tyrants such as Adolf Hitler, Emperor Hirohito, and Benito Mussolini. Young people eagerly enlisted to fight to protect our freedom and way of life from these vicious, cold-blooded dictators who wanted to rule the world. The men and women who went to war, under those circumstances, were revered as heroes. In contrast, the war in Viet Nam was perceived by many people of that era as a big travesty that was all about some dirty politics over money, oil, and power. Young people wondered, "What are we really fighting for anyway?" Even worse, those who did go to fight, willingly or not, were jeered by members of the anti-war movement upon their return to their own home country. That is, if they were fortunate enough to return alive. For those reasons, this war was one where I could not see myself eagerly signing up. I knew in my heart that I would fight to the death if our country was attacked by a dictator who wanted to conquer America, but at twelve-years old, I could not yet comprehend why it was necessary for our young men and women to die in jungles on the other side of the world fighting a country that never directly attacked us.

Anyway, I had a reprieve from this whole war nightmare when the Nixon administration did away with the draft in the early seventies, and I later headed off to college during the late seventies to learn about a wide range of subjects, including philosophy, religion, science, politics, and economics, just to name a few. But the dread I felt from living under the dark cloud of the Viet Nam War era still left its scar on me. In the early eighties, those trepidations were reignited as the cold war with Russia really heated up during the Reagan administration. The arms race escalated so badly that it seemed as if the whole issue over defense spending focused on which super-power had the arms to blow up the entire world more times than the other—although it only takes once for crying out loud! Reagan even commenced the Star Wars program, which involved the concept of having satellites circling the earth that would use laser beams to destroy inter-continental ballistic missiles (ICBMs) that might be fired at the United States.

I often thought, *"How badly can we possibly fear our fellow human beings here on earth that governments will take so many billions of the tax payers' hard-earned money and spend it on such insanity."* Later, I figured out that the Reagan administration really just played the Russians like a backboard. The strategy to spend them into submission, albeit by using citizen's tax dollars and unprecedented deficit spending to build frightening weapons of mass destruction, finally worked when Russia basically went broke around 1986 and was therefore forced to turn to democracy and an economic system of free enterprise. At least that's my own take on it, regardless of what a bona fide historian or economist might say.

However, I also had the distinct feeling that Reagan's defense secretary, Alexander Haig, AKA "Haig the Horrible," would have *truly* liked nothing more than to press that big, red doomsday button—for real! This belief, along with an ulterior motive of hearing some good music, prompted me to attend a massive anti-nuclear demonstration held in Central Park in New York City on June 12, 1982. It was estimated that about one million people showed up that day to protest against nuclear weapons and the Cold War arms' race. I didn't know it when I attended, but it was the largest anti-nuclear protest and also the largest political demonstration at a single location in U.S. history up to that point.

As I said before, life takes its toll and innocence fades. By 1990, the sixties were just a vague memory of a more innocent time that gave way to a more skittish society scarred by fear, and perhaps some bitterness, toward a government that had become progressively harder and harder to trust.

This next poem reflects my sentiments about life in the early eighties, living in the midst of such madness:

Devolution

The highest priest now laughs at praying
No one knows what the poet's saying
Politicians still play their games
But nothing else seems quite the same

Love is weeping, no more friends
Nuclear plants we just can't mend
Music nowhere can be heard
A cold sun shades the wilting birds

We thrive on drugs and late-night boozin'
On this eve of Devolution
Mad men rail at a blood-splattered moon
The demons of darkness shall reign here soon

The world is wheezing its final breath
Every road here leads to death
We scurry to live, but time has stopped
The party is over—The

bombs

have

dropped!!!!

Although I never did serve in any branch of the U.S. armed forces, I have always considered myself to be deeply patriotic. I love our country and the freedoms we all enjoy here. I am proud to call myself an American, although I may sometimes feel ashamed for some of the people who are in power in our government. However, whenever I hear a person vehemently deriding the government, particularly the federal government, my verbatim advice to them is, "Even if you don't believe in your government, you should still believe in your *country*."

I mentioned that my dad was a World War II veteran, but I didn't mention that he was also an attorney, and a staunch right-wing, conservative Republican. In short, I was none of the above. Although I refused to label myself either a Republican or Democrat, which is still true to this day, I behaved more like the young know-it-all liberal-minded punk, fresh out of college, who would debate with my dad enthusiastically about how Reagan's supply-side economics, or "Reaganomics," was a totally botched theory that would cause our country to go broke. I argued that his push for more and more tax cuts during a time of frivolous and out-of-control spending was just as insane as the administration's foreign policy and the arms race with Russia. We also crossed swords over the economics of war, in general. Since Dad grew up during the Great Depression era he was able to witness, first hand, the momentously rejuvenating impact that World War II had on the devastated American economy. Although the wartime economy propelled the United States from the darkest depths of economic and social despair it ever experienced, I also look at this as one of the worst possible side effects of any war ever. "Yeah, there's nothing like a good war to spur the economy and put people to work in the vast and powerful military-industrial complex," the old-timers like my dad would say. Well, that's just great! How can there ever be hope for having peace in this world when you have people, namely politicians and their corporate political hacks, drumming up wars because of the demonstrated economic benefits that can be realized? Although it was obviously an unintended and beneficial consequence of World War II, what is to stop the modern-day corporate war moguls and politicians from continually trying to use that knowledge to their advantage? This is a dilemma we face to this very day.

After getting frustrated arguing with me, Dad would often urge me to get involved and do something about it if I was so damn smart, and it bothered me so much. I may not have served in the military, but I took him up on his challenge to serve society. I found out quickly how your views can change when you are no longer watching from the sidelines and saying, "Why don't they just do *this*, or can't they just do *that?*" Things are a bit more complicated than they look from the outside observer's perspective. There is no "easy button" to press on either the right or the left.

One thing Dad and I did agree upon is that we live in a great country, and the people who run their mouths about it should either put up or shut up. So, I decided to become a public servant and put my talents to good use in the field of government finance. I became a Certified Public Finance Officer, and have been working in the field for more than thirty years now and have maintained a pretty good track record in keeping the governmental entities that I have served in very good financial health. I may not be fixing the global economy, but I am at least involved in doing my part in my own little corner of the world to make a difference. I'm not wealthy, but I'm happy and grateful for what I *do* have. I also have no problem getting up in the morning and facing myself in the mirror knowing that I work hard to earn an honest living serving the public. My uniform is a suit and tie, and my weapons are my computer, my brain, and my sincere desire and intent to do my absolute best for those I serve.

Another virtue that Dad and I agreed upon was the importance of having a good work ethic; to be willing to roll up your sleeves and work hard until a job gets done—and done *right*. Nothing is easy, and there are no free rides. If that's what you're looking for, then you are part of the problem in our society and not part of the solution. Of course, there are those who are legitimately entitled to government subsidies, such as disabled veterans and young children who were born into destitute conditions by no fault of their own.

Looking back over the course of history, we can recognize a pattern within social structures where the various members of a group or tribe of people each had their respective roles to play in contribution to the overall functioning and well-being of their societal unit. For instance, some may have had the responsibility of hunting or gathering food, while others were expected to prepare food, care for the young, build shelters, or assume other duties necessary to ensure the sustainability of their group. If members of the group became too old or sick to perform their role, the group would generally care for those people who dutifully performed their roles when they could. It is unlikely that any member of the group who deliberately avoided their duties, or who deceptively and greedily appropriated resources of the group for themselves, would be willingly cared for or accepted by the remainder of the group. Furthermore, it is likely that such freeloaders would have become social outcasts and eventually be banished from the group or face some other sort of punishment.

In modern American society, similar systems to those of the past have developed to care for the sick, disabled, and elderly who have contributed to society. These systems include Social Security and Medicare, as well as a variety of other social programs intended to assist the *truly* needy. Sadly, many people have found ways to take advantage of loopholes in such programs, or fraudulently apply for benefits of the program, often to the detriment of other deserving members of society. Although many conscionable Americans frown upon such practices, many others embrace them and even depend upon them as a way to get through life with minimal effort. They might even share their methods for taking advantage of the system with others and brag about their conquests. I strive not to be judgmental, but I share in the historical notion that if you are a healthy and capable person, but your modus operandi is to spend all day figuring out ways to "cheat the system" or rip people off, including our government coffers, then you might represent more of a threat to our way of life here in America than any other nation, religion, or political system on the planet, and should be dealt with accordingly. This threat is even more repugnant when those same "freeloaders" *use* children, the mentally ill, or the elderly as a reason for receiving a subsidy, but then spend it primarily for themselves. During my tenure working in the government sector, I have witnessed people from all walks of life participate in this common practice of "milking the system" regardless of race, religion, and even socio-economic status. When called out on it, they never blame themselves, but point fingers back to the "broken system." While it may be true that the system is broken in many ways, the mentality that one should just "milk" the system for whatever they can, particularly if lying, cheating, or deception is involved, is even more broken. I see the deterioration of respect and concern for upholding ethical and moral standards in American society to be a significant threat to our country and civilization, which accounts for my obvious passion on the subjects addressed in this chapter.

Ethics was once described to me by a college professor as the study of freedom versus responsibility, and the ability to strike the right balance between the two. In our country, we enjoy a great deal of freedom and with that freedom comes a great deal of responsibility. Without the proper balance between the two, the yin and the yang go off kilter and the whole country starts spinning out of control. It is like having a nuclear power plant, but not providing for any means to safely contain the radioactivity. Eventually, everything gets contaminated.

"America will never be destroyed from the outside. If we falter and lose our freedoms, it will be because we destroyed ourselves."

~ President Abraham Lincoln

In describing the premise of the book *Brave New World* in the Introduction of this book, I mentioned how leaders of the futuristic world order believed that the forfeiture of freedom and individuality within society was a small price to pay for maintaining social order, structure, and stability. It concerns me that world leaders, especially those here in the United States, may progressively move toward restricting our freedoms and individuality the more people within society shun responsibility and drift away from ethical and moral standards. This movement represents a social malady, which leaders may perceive as a severe and unacceptable threat to social stability.

Another aspect of American society I have deep concerns about and involves practically all Americans is the great divide between Republicans and Democrats. The majority of Americans have taken sides and labeled themselves as either a Republican or Democrat. I have observed that most people tend to defend their position rather strongly and often passionately. It also appears to me that more energy is spent by politicians in both parties on making each other look bad than on working together to make America look good, and explaining how they propose to accomplish that. In fact, I find it downright embarrassing how we air our dirty laundry on the world stage through the media by way of editorials, negative campaign ads, social media posts, and derogatory speeches that persistently and scathingly condemn the particular views of each of the opposing political parties and insult their respective supporters. It sends a message out to the rest of the world that the United States of America is not actually united—far from it. One of the most primitive tactics of warfare is to "divide and conquer." Well, our enemies are already halfway there. We've already taken care of the "divide" part for them. Americans ought to start working harder to find some common ground lest Abraham Lincoln's prophecy comes true.

This great chasm in the political landscape of America is near the top of my list of reasons for loathing labels. Once an individual, especially a politician, labels themselves as either a Republican or a Democrat, or liberal or conservative, they have painted themselves into a corner where they either go along with *all* the basic principles of their party affiliation, or run the risk of being derided for being a hypocrite or a traitor to their party. This means that, even if it's very clear what the right thing to do is, they will be strongly inclined not do it if it doesn't conform to their party's norms, principles, or values. For instance, if it is clear that a tax increase is needed to maintain service levels at minimum levels expected or demanded by the majority of the citizenry, Republican politicians would still most likely not be supportive of it. What would their constituents think of a Republican who actually dared to support a tax hike?! Likewise, if spending on some social program is clearly not working and proven to be purely wasteful spending, the Democrats may not be likely to support cutting funding for the program because of the same reason; they don't want that on their voting record because it is inconsistent with the ideals of the political party they chose to associate themselves with.

Even worse, I have observed that there is a tendency for the two parties not to support many of their opponent's ideas or legislative proposals no matter how clever, brilliant, or beneficial they think they might be for the citizenry as a whole. When one party loses an election and their representative stands there proclaiming that they will support the winning party and move forward in a unified fashion, I find it very hard to believe them. It seems to me that there is an ongoing fear that if the party who is in power proves to be immensely successful, that could spell disaster for the party who is not in power. Why would anybody ever want to vote out the successful incumbents when things are going so well? That being the case, how can we ever have a government that is cooperative and not dysfunctional with this sort of combative relationship prevailing between the two parties? Then throw in the fact that there is big money being poured into campaigns by huge corporations that also have the deep pockets to pay for attorneys and lobbyists to support their interests, and we have one big mess on our hands.

So, in the end, it is the vast majority of the citizenry who suffers. What most politicians don't seem to realize is that there are a lot of voters who really don't give a rat's rump about their individual voting records on specific issues if, by the end of their term, they can prove through economic and other indicators that the results of their collective decisions were positive, effectual, and beneficial to society as a whole. Of course, the media fuels this fire, but my perception is that both parties spend way too much time and energy trying to kick each other in the proverbial crotch instead of setting their egos aside and simply doing the right thing, which is doing *whatever* it takes to get the job done and do the best they can for *all* the citizens and the *entire* society that they serve. Instead, they often just spin their wheels, frustrating each other and the citizenry alike, and getting very little accomplished. Even worse, whatever accomplishments *are* made are played down or even flat-out denied by the opposing party.

I, for one, have grown weary of experiencing the "Divided States of America" created by this dichotomy. And who isn't totally fed up with those incessant and obnoxious negative campaign ads also? Forget Halloween—they are the true horror just prior to the November elections.

Let's face it; there have been both Republican and Democratic administrations that have left us with a bad taste in our mouths because of the way things have been handled. Fortunately, though, we have the freedom and privilege to speak up and state our opinions about our gripes with the government without the fear of being imprisoned or having our heads cut off. We also have the right to vote for someone else, as opposed to having a dictator appointed for us. So, when I hear people totally trash the United States and say how they are so fed up and disgusted that they want to move away to another country, I remind them of these things. I also tell them something that I mentioned previously, but I feel is important enough to reiterate. Even if they don't believe in our government, they should still believe in our *country*. Not to mention, you can always choose to get involved and try to make a difference, at least in your own little corner of the world. Not every man or woman may be cut out to be a politician, or to serve in the military or other public service, but everyone can choose to contribute to society in a positive and productive way based upon whatever talents they *do* have to offer. Speaking up is important, but to merely engage in hurtful name-calling, whining, and bickering is counterproductive. I see it as a responsibility of all truly patriotic Americans to simply stop fostering this destructive pattern of behavior that is weakening our country.

"I've had it with the right; I've had it with the left. I've had it with the sleepers who blame the government."

I think Uncle Sam has stepped into enough piles of elephant and donkey pooh along the path of democracy and freedom. In fact, we now have it splattered all over us—and it looks and smells awful!!! I strongly believe that until those differences are reconciled and this type of behavior ceases, our government will continue to appear foolish, ineffectual, and dysfunctional to both Americans and citizens abroad and will put a big damper on the flame beneath our melting pot.

"Let us not seek the Republican answer or the Democratic answer, but the right answer. Let us not seek to fix the blame for the past. Let us accept our own responsibility for the future."

~ John F. Kennedy

This next poem reflects my feelings about how our great nation can only be kept on the right track if we would just get back to the fundamental principles of our forefathers and early settlers and show some sincere humility and determination and work together as a united nation:

Rekindling the Dream

Ego trips and power flips
Paranoia city
Too many gangs and homos—
They'll need a new committee

The flame beneath the melting pot
Smolders now in ashes
Ghettos, groups and factions
Are dividing all the masses

Commies make their comeback,
Neo-Nazis raging
But there's another war these days
That Uncle Sam is waging

He's homeless now and hungry
And his shadow scares him most
For it's been growing ever longer—
Sun is setting on our host

Who'll run the bed and breakfast
That will put him up at dawn?
It's the people of his nation
Tearing up the White House lawn

Don't forget the recipe
Our forefathers devised
It's not the one of soup kitchens
Or even apple pie

Leave your ego on the shelf
Rejoice in liberation
Humility can spark the fire
Of true determination

The flame beneath the melting pot
Is stoked by True Desire
The fire of ol' Miss Liberty
Reaching ever higher!

Imagining a world without religion may be an extremely hard concept for many to comprehend and a real tough pill to swallow, but I have absolutely no problem imaging a country without two political parties that will continue to bang heads for centuries to come. Although I feel it is unlikely that I will see the two-party system eliminated in my lifetime, I remain hopeful that people will wise-up to the fact that the differences of the two parties desperately need to be reconciled and the extreme positions of each be moderated to the point where we see acceptable levels of compromise and cooperation. Wouldn't it be nice to know that at the conclusion of a presidential election we are not left with approximately half of the citizenry having a feeling of defeat, despair, and hopelessness? That is exactly what happened in 2012, 2016, and many times before. If it doesn't feel right, there's a good chance that it really *isn't* right. When a country gets fed up with the administration of one party, we usually see a wholesale change where people will vote straight down the ballot along party lines for the opposite party. This applies even when people have absolutely no idea about who they are voting for, and they may even unwittingly vote for candidates who don't even support any of their interests. The only real concern of this kind of voter is if a candidate is a Republican or a Democrat, or if the candidate portrays an image that they identify with, so that's how they vote. This often causes a sudden and drastic change literally overnight, which could lead to a period of instability and weakness until everything shakes out. By the time all the dust settles—if it ever does—it's time for another election.

In keeping with the liberating philosophy of Jeet Kune Do, to use no way as way and have no limitations as limitations, I have flip-flopped back and forth and voted for both Republican and Democratic candidates at all levels of government according to my understanding of how those candidates stood in relation to the issues that meant the most to me at the time. That is the best-case scenario. Sadly, I also found myself having to choose based on who I thought would cause the least damage. Personally, I'm more concerned about how far one is to the right or the left.

Being either too liberal or too conservative can have more serious consequences, in my estimation, than which political party they belong to. The important thing is to exercise your right to vote and not to *fear* a candidate based upon their party affiliation. We must then follow up by holding them accountable by voicing either our pleasure or discontent with any of their actions. If they are really bad, then vote them out, write your Congressman, or take other action to help bring about change; don't just lie down, roll over, and give up.

Since the 2016 presidential election, our nation has been faced with one of the most dangerously divided electorates in the history of our nation, at least that I have ever experienced or learned of. Unless swift action is taken by both citizens and leaders of our nation, I have grave concerns that this situation may degenerate into a situation similar to what we had during the Civil War, or even worse.

One thing I have learned is that having a good understanding of the concept of public problems, values, and choices can really help to bring people who are at extreme opposite ends of the political spectrum much closer to the middle where they could at least hold civil and healthy debate about various issues rather than just viciously and maliciously attacking one another.

An example of a public problem would be the case of a manufacturing corporation that is complaining about being unfairly burdened with environmental regulations imposed by the government, which are cutting into their profits and preventing them from hiring more employees and expanding their operations. In fact, there are people living in nearby neighborhoods who say they used to work at the manufacturing facility but had been laid off after management was forced to comply with costly regulatory requirements that were imposed upon them by government agencies. Stockholders also complain that the value of their holdings have taken a hit as soon as news of the regulations was made public when they hadn't even been implemented yet. The values that all these stakeholders in the company hold dear are their freedom to conduct business as they wish without the government interfering with their operations, as well as the values of individual rights and prosperity. Republicans and conservatives tend to gravitate toward supporting this particular set of values and laissez-faire policy.

However, there is another public problem with this situation. People living in the nearby neighborhoods also claim that prior to those regulations being imposed, they were constantly plagued with the problems of loud noise and unbearable smells of toxic fumes being produced by operations at the plant. There had also been reports of toxic chemicals being buried on the property that were having a very dangerous impact on the water table as the toxins seeped down into the earth, posing another serious public health problem. Doctors and other health officials even linked instances of cancer and other serious illnesses occurring within the vicinity of the plant directly to those same toxins. Therefore, the values that those people hold dear are those of health, safety, environmental protection, well-being, and quality of life; values commonly defended by Democrats and liberals.

So, how do we solve these public problems fairly? Obviously, some choices need to be made in regard to solving the dilemma of these conflicting values. Both groups have valid arguments and are entitled to hold certain values in higher regard than others. One cannot clearly and honestly claim that one side is totally right, and the other side is totally wrong. However, that is exactly what we see all too often when radically right and radically left people argue over such matters. They will completely fail to see the validity of each other's arguments and try to dismiss them or discredit their sources of information as fake news. Moreover, many people seem to only want to read or listen to arguments that support their own beliefs or fit their personal narrative. They might even seek out such arguments to gain reassurance and reinforcement of their beliefs and strongly avoid and ignore cases and facts to the contrary, no matter how clear and indisputable they may be. This tendency is not only common amongst the citizenry but also amongst politicians and other public officials who are looked upon to be an intermediary and make those tough choices and decisions. We are often failed by them to make those tough choices because they feel they must support the values that are dominant amongst the majority of the constituents who elected them and fear for their political futures if they show any pity or support for the values of "the other side."

So long as such a destructive and divisive mindset persists, the very fabric of our society will continue to fade and be torn apart to the point that we will be exceedingly weak and vulnerable to our *real* enemies around the world, who will surely use this tragic state of affairs to their advantage. Divide and conquer. It is bad enough to watch this spectacle unfold within the ranks of our various levels of government amongst the politicians, but as this cancer spreads more and more into the grassroots of our nation—we the people—it becomes a lethal social disease to which our nation will eventually succumb. Sadly, I have personally experienced the ill effects of this insidious and treacherous malady and painfully witnessed the disintegration of both friendships and family relations. It even creeps its way into the workplace, churches, and other public settings where people congregate or socialize. It is up to us, and I mean all of us, to stay educated, open-minded, and not allow this degeneration of relationships to happen, especially within the family unit—the very foundation of society.

Earlier, I explained how naming and labeling causes fear and how fear leads to hatred. The common practice of labeling ourselves as liberals, conservatives, Republicans, or Democrats is a classic case-in-point. Also recall the analogy of the usefulness of the cup in its emptiness. Empty your cup! Use no way as way and have no limitations as limitations. A wise former boss of mine used to always say, *"The truth is the hardest commodity to come by."* It is up to us to put our fears and prejudices aside and seek out the truth. As illustrated by the foregoing example, there may be truth to what we believe, but is it the whole truth and nothing but the truth? That is the question we need to constantly ask ourselves if there is to be any meaningful reconciliation, healing, or true patriotic brotherhood within our society. The act of calling oneself a "true patriot" while advocating for mass genocide of those who don't think like you is nothing but true absurdity. Failure to recognize that our own thoughts and opinions are not the only way to view things is nothing but sheer arrogance.

Another aspect of government I find very disturbing and potentially destructive is when the rules of separation of church and state are blatantly broken. As citizens of the United States, our forefathers afforded us the freedom of studying and practicing any religion we choose without interference from the government, per the First Amendment to the Constitution. As mentioned earlier, I attended a public school but went through the process of becoming a confirmed Catholic completely outside of the public schools I attended. I don't think it would have been fair or proper if, for instance, I was forced to learn Judaism in my public, tax-funded grammar school because a majority of students who attended were Jewish. As it turns out, I did end up studying Judaism while attending Providence College—a private college founded by Dominican Friars—but that was my own choice, and it was at my own expense. Conversely, I don't think it would have been fair to either the students or their tax-paying parents if all those Jewish students in my grammar school were forced to learn about Christianity had the school board been mandated to teach it by a higher level of government. The same holds true for students of any other religion if we are to be fair and treat citizens of all denominations equally, as our forefathers advocated.

In short, when the government gets involved in religion to the point where they interfere by ramming the tenets of a *particular* faith down the throats of Americans who don't follow the mandated creed, it becomes a very slippery slope. I find it disconcerting how some politicians and others in our society express intense fear over the notion of America becoming dominated by Islam, but the same people would not think twice about forcing Christianity upon *all* people within our very religiously diverse society. This is simply irrational, hypocritical, and contrary to the very principles that our great nation was founded upon, and some would surely argue it is unconstitutional. Although I would strongly agree that *true* Christian values do play a very big and important role within American society for many people, I don't think it would be right for the government to declare America a Christian nation and, thereby, force Christianity upon all citizens no matter what creed they follow, if they even follow one. Given our diverse culture, this could only cause resentment and more fear, which only fuels the fire of hatred. It could make enemies of people within our society who we would have otherwise been able to coexist peacefully with, had they been left alone to freely practice their own religion without such an imposition or interference. Just to be very clear, by "freely" I do not mean having the right to commit any acts of cruelty, violence, or abuse. The last I checked, acts such as public beatings and stoning people to death are not legal in any state in the United States, and I don't see the laws that prohibit such actions being repealed anytime soon, nor would I ever advocate such a thing. If acts of violence such as those practiced by some religions ever did become legal here in America, we would have much bigger problems, and I would be one of the first ones to hightail it out of here.

As previously established, both the *Holy Bible* and the *Quran* refer to such violent and harmful acts as forms of punishment, so shouldn't we fear either one having a strong influence on American government? Although stoning and public beatings are essentially a thing of the past for Christianity, but not for all of Islamic faith, it doesn't mean these cruel forms of punishment can *never* be brought back, especially if living under an authoritarian government dominated by Christian religious *extremists*. This notion may seem far-fetched to many, but it is really not out of the realm of possibility, which is a big reason why I believe in the separation of church and state. We need the government to keep the violent aspects of religious fanaticism in check as much as we need to seek benefit from the peaceful and virtuous aspects of religion that may help to keep any unscrupulous politicians and others in government in check. We also need to be mindful of the fact that it is not below some politicians to use, or should I say *abuse,* religion to appeal to the faithful and gain their votes and support; don't be fooled by such posers!

I can easily see how Christians here in America would be quick to jump on the bandwagon and cheer on politicians advocating for their religion to be declared the official religion of the country, thereby making it the dominant one with full endorsement by the U.S government. Again, I think it is important for those people to set aside their personal prejudices for a moment and think about some of their friends, neighbors, or workmates who worship a different religion, and imagine how such a declaration might feel to them. When one religion is declared to be dominant or "official" by the government, is that not saying that all other religions are subordinate and inferior, at least in the eyes of the government? Would that not give the more radical Christian religious fanatics a sense of empowerment and embolden them to harass people of other faiths? How does this promote equality, liberty, and justice for all, which is what our country is supposed to stand for? There are those who believe that a true separation of church and state is just not possible and may even *fear* such a separation, but which state of affairs is truly worse? In America, I believe it is important that the government be perceived as religiously neutral and do all that it can to see that U.S. citizens of all different religious faiths are treated as equally and fairly as possible, in accordance with the First Amendment. Likewise, people of all religions, especially those who come here seeking to start a new life free from tyranny and oppression, need to respect the American principles and values of law, order, life, liberty, equality, and civility if they ever want to successfully assimilate into our society. If this is *truly* understood, there is nothing to fear.

As we look back through the annals of history, we can see countless examples of how fear has triggered incidents of violence, conflict, and war. In many instances, the outbreaks of violence were unavoidable and arguably justified, such as the defensive actions taken against Adolf Hitler and the Third Reich. Even the *New Testament* speaks of Michael the Archangel who led God's army in the war against Satan's forces that is described in the Book of Revelation. As long as there is evil in the world that poses a true and legitimate threat to anyone or anything that is good, we can count on there being more conflict and violence.

I recall back when I worked in my first government job in the early eighties; I used to squabble with my textbook conservative Republican boss over the policies of the Reagan administration. Sometimes those disputes rivaled the ones I had with my dad, especially spats over the subject of the arms race with Russia. He argued vehemently that there could never be world peace because, "War is a thing of *passion*!" I worried he might have a stroke when he proclaimed that foreboding prophecy because when he said the word "passion," he suddenly clenched his fist up in the air and his wild-eyed face turned beet-red, with vitriolic spit flying like shrapnel from his raging mouth. That verbal exchange and image obviously left a strong impression on me since I am now writing about it more than thirty years later. The concept of world peace is a good one, but how do we even begin to *realistically* achieve global serenity? We can start with setting our intentions on trust, love, and a bit of *guarded* optimism, but at the same time always being mindful of the fact that evil still lurks all around us and sometimes even *within* us.

Our lack of trust in our fellow man can cause us to behave very irrationally and do things that are very hurtful to others and to ourselves. Granted, some of this comes from past experiences. For example, a black person may be very mistrustful and resentful of white people because of the historical reality of slavery and discrimination in our country. Likewise, a white person may be fearful and mistrustful of blacks because he or she perceives them to be angry and hateful of whites because of the history of discrimination, even whites who had nothing to do with and abhor the practice of slavery or discrimination. Of course, racial conflict is a much more complicated matter, but I want to provide a simplified illustration of how it can be an incessant vicious cycle. At some point, there needs to be acceptance and forgiveness—by *both* sides—or it never ends.

"Without forgiveness, there's no future."

~Desmond Tutu

The phenomenon of lack of trust does not just occur between racial groups, but also between people of different religions, political groups, and nationalities. It happens with anyone who is different from us, and we perceive as a threat—a threat to our way of life, a threat to our beliefs and conventions, a threat to our property, or a threat to our physical safety. The key word in the previous sentence is "perceived." The threat does not even need to be real or imminent. So long as we think it, it can cause us to react defensively and perhaps irrationally, and could cause that which we fear to happen, even if it wasn't about to happen. It's the self-fulfilling prophecy. For instance, if a person is mistrustful and fearful of people of Middle Eastern descent because of the events of 9-11, they might do something irrational like tackle an Iranian guy on an airplane if they see him walking briskly toward the front of the plane. It may then turn out that the guy was a U.S. Air Marshal, heading to the restroom in a big hurry and ends up taking out the fear-monger who tackled him because he assumed that *he* was a terrorist.

"I am an American patriot not because I was born here, but because I was not."

~ Khizir Khan (Muslim-American Gold Star father of U.S. Army captain Humayun Khan, killed in Baquba, Iraq in 2004 by a suicide bomber)

In reading the title to this chapter, "We're Not Gun-A Take It!" some of you might have thought about the song by glam metal band Twisted Sister that had a similar title. The band's front-man, Dee Snider, was one of several famous characters who attended the same high school as me in Baldwin, New York, and someone for whom I have immense respect because of his crusade against censorship. Although the theme of that signature song of theirs is obviously rooted in rebellion, I was referring to words uttered by a different colorful character. He was a fictitious newscaster from the film *Network* who became particularly perturbed about the unruly and out-of-control state of affairs in our society. He urged everybody to stick their heads out of their windows and shout out to the world that they were mad as hell and not going to take this anymore!

Having grown up in New York, I could appreciate exactly what that character was ranting and raving about. I originally wrote this poem about New York City, but it could be any old gritty city.

Gritty City

I jumped off the cross-town bus
On the east side of the city
Choked a breath of urban air and
Strut down sidewalk gritty

People staring straight ahead
As I pass them in the night
I guess it's hard to say "hello"
While trembling with fright

Stumbling over drooling bums
On concrete beds of slime,
I tossed a buck to an old bag lady
Begging for a dime

As I made it to the subway station
It was hard to find it funny
When a dude disguised as a meter maid
Demanded all my money!

I took a train to the end of the line
Drinking away self-pity
As I thought about what lunacy
Abides in Gritty City

Although following the advice of blowing off steam by hollering out your window that you're "mad as hell and not going to take this anymore" probably won't do any good at all, and might even cause your neighbors to call the cops on you, I often think about how true it is that so many people have basically "stuck their head in the sand" and callously tune out the ugly side of humanity that is all-too-often puked out all over us by the media. As I sat writing this, the eleven o'clock news came on, and I heard about a shooting at a court house, a school shooting, a cop shot dead while dealing with a domestic quarrel, and an outbreak of violence on a commuter train in Atlanta. It's easy to become numb to such news, especially when it's all you ever hear about on a daily basis.

But while all that pervasive madness was going on in the world, I'm sure that there were also a lot of good things happening as well. Certainly, volunteers were out helping the homeless and the hungry, scientists were busy making amazing new discoveries, and artists were passionately creating or composing breathtaking masterpieces. If I tend to tune out all the violence I hear about through the media, it's not because I'm apathetic or indifferent to it. It is because I am busy searching for all that *good* news that I know is out there. I prefer to spend my time doing that, as opposed to going down to the gun range to make sure I am prepared to deal with the big "race war" anticipated by so many. I have no objections to the right of Americans to do that, if they want to, but I'm too busy observing and writing about all the amazing things going on in our world and the universe. Although I am careful and vigilant because of true and valid *concerns* about safety and security, I refuse to allow myself to be obsessed with fear and *worry* that an oppressive and dysfunctional government—or anybody—might suddenly bust down my door and seize all my possessions, revoke all my rights, or worse. Why torture myself with such wearisome suffering?

"When the power of love overcomes the love of power,
the world will know peace."

~ Jimi Hendrix

Once we allow our lives to be controlled by fear, we have opened the door to all the chaos and disorder that we fear. On the flip side, if we decide to allow our lives to be controlled by love and have some faith in the goodness of our fellow humans and have good intent and practice good deeds, such as helping others in need, we then open the door to serenity, order, and bliss. If you want to put a label on this concept of causality, you could call it Karma, but that's just a word. It's really just very simple—what goes around comes around, as the old adage goes. Despite the obvious hypocrisy when compared to the *Quran* verse I referenced earlier that advocates beheading people, there is also valuable wisdom in the following verse:

"Whoever recommends and helps a good cause
becomes a partner therein, and whoever recommends
and helps an evil cause shares in its burdens"

~ Quran:4:85

You might even note a striking similarity in the following *Bible* verse:

"A man reaps what he sows."

~ Galatians 6:7

Some also refer to this concept as the law of attraction. If you hold onto negative thoughts and feelings, or expose yourself to being influenced by the negative thoughts of others, then your tendency will be to put negative vibrations out into the world and thereby attract negativity to yourself. Conversely, if you hold only positive thoughts and feelings in your mind, and stay in the company of people who also think positive thoughts, then those good vibrations will emanate from you and will attract goodness back to yourself. It's a simple but powerful concept with very broad application. You can attract just about anything you want, if you just truly focus your mind, heart, and soul on it. Think it, feel it, be it. Don't believe me? Try it!

The Mirror

Even though your frown won't shine
It casts a clear reflection
Off of every face it meets
And comes in your direction

And all the rotten trash you spread
About everyone you know
Soon will have you smelling ripe
From head down to your toe

All the world's a mirror
And regardless of your place
Everything you do and say
Gets thrown back in your face

Don't you sit and wonder
Why you're always getting burned
When half of all the love you take
Never gets returned

Try living with a smile
And you'll soon find out it's true
That all the happy vibes you send
Will find their way to you

All the world's a mirror
And our image won't erase
The way we treat each other
Will reflect the human race

"And so even though we face the difficulties of today and tomorrow, I still have a dream."

~ Martin Luther King, Jr.

Given the state of affairs in our world today, I am not so naïve to think that we can completely drop our guard and leave our doors unlocked or our keys in our car. But to live in constant fear and sit guard by our windows and doors with a loaded gun just waiting, or even worse, *hoping* for the opportunity to blow away an intruder does not represent the quality of life that appeals to me. I can and am willing to defend myself and my property, but the one thing I refuse to ever be robbed of is my peace of mind and my general sense of good will and faith in humanity.

Whether you are an evolutionist who believes that we all came from the same cosmic dust of the stars, or a creationist who believes that we are all descendants of Adam and Eve, there is still the common note that we are all related—somehow. I choose not to fear my relatives. We are all indigenous people of the planet Earth.

"If we have no peace, it is because we have forgotten that we belong to each other."

~ Mother Teresa

Flocks of a Bird

There's only one reality
A part of which that we can see
The things we miss you'll find in others
That is why they call us brothers

There's only one true human race
Soaring high upon this place
Different folks are birds of a feather
Flocks of a bird are we together

There's only one real Happiness
Everlasting song of bliss
Spirits are rising with the sun
A new day's dawning
We are one

*"And crown thy good with brotherhood from sea to
shining sea."*

~ Katharine Lee Bates

America is one of the greatest experiments of all time—
*Conceived in liberty and dedicated to the proposition that all men are created
equal.* How I wish that *all* Americans would truly understand and
appreciate those words and actually live by them. How wonderful
would it be if that doctrine came to be a global commitment? I
imagine there will always be those who will read things like this
and initially think, "Yeah, keep on dreaming, Mister John
Lennon-Kennedy." But then again, I also do imagine that I am
not alone in my hope and faith in humanity. Won't you please
join us? If the vast majority of people in the world begin thinking
this way, the fearful haters and war-mongers of the world will

eventually be defused and relegated to an ineffectual minority position. This may be the best we could ever hope for, but I'd take it in a heartbeat.

"There is no fear in love."

~ John 4:18

Gun-to-Rose by Laura Davis

CHAPTER FIVE
A MATTER OF LIFE AND DEATH

"As a well-spent day brings happy sleep, so a life well used brings happy death."

~ Leonardo da Vinci, Italian polymath (1452 - 1519)

What is life? That is the age-old question that man has pondered, ad nauseam, since ancient times. Perhaps a more perplexing and monumental question that man has contemplated and debated over the course of recorded history is the question of what is in store for us after we reach the end of our lives? These are two of the biggest mysteries surrounding our very existence here on earth. So, what are the best answers? Many of the devout, God-fearing people of the world might simply explain that we were given our lives by God and are expected to live our lives by His Ten Commandments. Those who strive to live by them and are repentant for their sins are rewarded upon death by acceptance into Heaven, and those who don't are condemned to either purgatory or that really bad place down below.

At the other end of the spectrum are people who believe that life here on earth is merely a chance freak of nature that we just have to deal with until we die, and then there is absolutely nothing that follows. Then there are a variety of other "in-between" ideologies, many of which suggest the existence of some sort of

Source energy, Creator, Sacred Power, Great Spirit, or other universal life force or consciousness that we all originated from, and will eventually return to, in the form of "conscious" energy or "soul" that maintains some degree of awareness depending upon how we lived our lives on earth.

The faithful religious find great comfort in their belief of salvation and eternal life in the Kingdom of Heaven, while people of the other extreme, such as atheists, believe that those religious people are just kidding themselves and have been "brainwashed" to believe those things just so they can go on living their lives with a false sense of comfort and security instead of facing the harsh reality of a godless existence that ends in nothingness. So, in the end, who will be surprised? Perhaps both will be?

No matter what you believe, there remains the reality that we are here on an amazing journey through a tiny window of time and space on a planet that has existed—according to scientists—for more than four and a half billion years, but only supported human life for a tiny fraction of that time. According to Carl Sagan's Cosmic Calendar, which views existence since the Big Bang as a single calendar year, civilized humans have only existed during the last seconds of the last minute of the last day of the year. Depending upon our perspective on the human condition, life could be either a true blessing that we take full advantage of or a horrible curse that we wish would just end soon—the sooner the better. We get to decide. I choose the former.

Laughing on the Run

A slick cat silver stares at the moon
Rising bright and proud
A little red sliver of a setting sun
Still peeking through the clouds

Throughout the woods around the lake
Nocturnal creatures chant
The whistling wind is right in tune
And the starlit shadows dance

This placid night, the feeling's right
A vacuum fills my mind
I've got a magic, mystic glow
A sage can't even find

We're living in an hourglass
The time is getting late
But I'll be laughing on the run
Life is more than great

"Some people are so afraid to die that they never begin to live."

~ Henry Van Dyke, American short-story writer, poet, and essayist (1852 - 1933)

As each day passes, I constantly remind myself to feel a strong and genuine sense of gratitude for all that I have. If you stop and pay close attention you will realize how much there really is to be grateful for, and the more grateful you feel, the more it will enrich your life more than anything else you can do for yourself. It's all too often that we take even the simplest things in life for granted, like a deep breath of fresh air, the warm sun on our bodies, the rain that brings us water, or the food on the shelves of a grocery store, let alone a dear friend or loved one. The list goes on and on, but all too often many of those things are either taken for granted or go completely unnoticed. I have found that the more I take notice of those things, and truly appreciate them, the better I feel about myself, others, and the whole world in which I live.

Conversely, one of the worst things you could ever do is to feel that you have nothing to be grateful for, and to constantly feel sorry for yourself. That is when people fall into a deep, dark abyss that they are lucky to ever pull themselves out of. Granted, that sort of mindset may sometimes be brought on by some sort of chemical imbalance or other legitimate physical or psychological malady, but sometimes people just flat-out give up on life. They may simply feel they will never be good enough for their family or never get the promotion they deserve or lose that weight or win the love of someone they truly adore. If this conviction persists for too long, and goes unchecked, they might eventually reach the point of no return. It's like entering the event horizon of a black hole; they get hopelessly drawn in and are lost forever.

"Where there is love there is life."

~ Indira Gandhi

There are different stages of living life in such darkness, and we probably have all experienced some degree of gloom, distress, or misfortune at some time along the journey of life. I know I certainly have experienced my fair share of sorrow, hardship, and suffering. I have accepted that those things are sometimes a very natural part of life, such as grieving over the loss of a loved one, but I have also learned to be very aware of my emotions when such darkness sets in. I fight to find the strength and positive energy to shake it off and pull myself out of it. In fact, I just took a two-week break from writing this book because I just felt I needed some time to recover from a string of recent personal and work experiences that left me feeling a bit drained emotionally. A balance needs to be maintained—the yin and the yang.

However, I have also known other people who were not quite as fortunate when it came to finding the inner strength to pull themselves up out of the dark, dirty ditches in which they fell. You may have heard expressions before such as, "*You need to either make dust or eat dust*," or, "*In this life, you need to either sink or swim.*" Both seem to imply some sort of strife in order to get along, but again I recall the analogy of going with the flow like a cork in a stream that gently bobs around all obstacles.

The following three poems are dedicated to all those who know and understand suffering, and to those I personally knew who never came back from the "black hole." I understand they may be a bit on the dark side and disturbing to some, but they were inspired by people and events that had a profound impact on me and motivated me to write.

Futility

The blindness of a tyrant
Is the sage's deepest fear
For the wholesome songs of wisdom
Will befall hard-deafened ears
That won't ever want to hear

In the drought of artful nectar
Fertile tillers leave their farms
In the shadow of a moment
The enlightened raise their arms
How a futile spirit harms!

Through the darkest evil valley
This old raging river winds
Coldly drowning out the silence
Washing peace out of our minds
Leaving sunken dreams behind

Hopeless

He tried to reach back in his head
He found a lot of brain cells dead
He fell and crumbled on the floor
He don't know how to love no more

See the fragile flower grow
See the wind—a fatal blow
See the day and want to cry
See the world and want to die

There's no more use in crying out
There's no more kid to sour out
There's no more zeal to take a dare
There's no one left who even cares

When all is dark and caving in
When it all but kills you just to grin
When to the trash your soul is tossed
When life is hopeless, all is lost

Short and Sweet Eulogy for Pete

So now you've left your mark
White shadow in the dark
Naught to want for in this life
Your golden heart felt pain and strife
No worse a fate in life there be
Than to long for one's mortality

Deafened by screams from the past
Echoed off walls of the future
Now there's silence
At last

"Forgive yourself before you die. Then forgive others."

~ Morrie Schwartz, American educator and writer (1916 - 1995)

One of the reasons for me taking a break from writing, as I referred to above, was the occurrence of a death in my family. Most people find it hard enough to think about the subject of death, let alone to discuss it or write about it. Because of my strong belief in an afterlife, I didn't think it would be so hard to write about death, but I found it's not that easy after all. It dredged up some bad memories for me, like the loss of my good friend who became despondent and decided to end his own life. Everybody loses a loved one through natural causes at some point in life, whether it be our grandparents, parents, aunts, and uncles, but sometimes we also have the misfortune of experiencing the loss of someone in a more untimely and tragic way. Those are the ones that catch us off-guard and hit us the hardest. Besides my friend who I wrote about above, I also remember grieving over the death of my sister's eighteen-year old boyfriend who died in a drowning accident when I was about fifteen years old. Later on, in my twenties, I lost a close friend, who was only twenty-seven, in a motorcycle accident, and also an ex-girlfriend, Laurie, who died of cancer.

Laurie was one of the people I knew who had a near-death experience and came back to tell about it. While we were dating, she told me about a time she had gone to the beach with some of her friends and went swimming out in some rough surf. A wave had knocked her over and held her under for a few seconds while she struggled to get her footing. Just as she stood up and gasped for air, another wave smacked her right in the kisser, and it was "lights out." Her friends noticed her limp body floating face down in the water and rushed to pull her out. She told me that she remembered floating around above the beach "like a seagull" and looking down and just watching while people worked on resuscitating her.

Since then, I was really fascinated with the whole concept of out-of-body experiences, and what really happens to us when our bodies cease to function. There were other experiences that made a believer out of me also. Just recently, a friend, Ali, returned from a trip to Dubai, and we met to play golf. Afterwards, we were sitting and chatting over a cold beverage, and he said he had to tell me about something that happened while he was away.

He told me he had been visiting with his brother and cousin, and while they were out during the night, a scuffle broke out. To make a long story short, he and his brother got caught up in the fracas, and he ended up dislocating his shoulder. When they brought him to the hospital he was in terrible pain, so he was given a shot of morphine. That didn't take care of the pain, so they gave him another shot, which also did not work so they finally decided to give him anesthesia to put him under and reset his shoulder.

While Ali was under anesthesia, he said that he remembered floating above the earth's atmosphere in what seemed to be a big white cloud. He assumed this was just a dream and never thought of it being anything other than a dream. He and everyone else around him existed in the form of balls of light that moved around at lightning speed. He also had waves of insight and wisdom that just came to him, as if all information was downloaded into him like a microchip in a computer. There was no verbal communication between him and the others; however, he knew everything by simply thinking internally about the question and quickly the answer came to him.

Below this cloud were many planets and atmospheres. Ali felt his experience/dream lasted eighteen hours while he experienced the utmost purity, humility, and happiness. As he shot around the cloud as a light figure, Ali remembers asking himself three questions with the answers provided right away. His questions were:

1. Am I dead? Your body is dead on earth. You are the soul.
2. Where am I? You are in the first level of heaven, a temporary place until judgment day when everyone in this level will enter the upper levels of heaven.

Ali also knew that he and the other light figures were lucky to be in this place because there was another place which was hell. He explained hell was not a fire or a place where devils poked you with sharp objects. He explained hell was a place where souls fell in a dark bottomless tunnel that never ended. Those souls were in fear as they fell in the never ending dark tunnel hoping to die but as they reach the floor, the floor drops lower, and they continue to fall.

3. Will there be peace in my homeland (Palestine) and when?
   Yes, within ten years. Palestinians will have their rights back and a state of their own.

Ali said in addition to the already-known information, these are the only three questions he internally asked with the information given to him right away.

After what seemed to be eighteen hours of tranquility, Ali remembers getting sucked down out of the cloud by a very strong magnet-like energy. Ali fought very hard to stay in the cloud as he knew this was the energy taking him back to earth, and ultimately, back to his body. This episode took several minutes as Ali internally requested that he not return to earth, to his body, but stay in this place in his current form, but that was internally rejected. Suddenly, Ali woke up and saw four or five doctors, his brother, and his cousin standing over his bed.

Everyone in the room was quiet except for Ali because he could not stop talking about the most beautiful, peaceful, and euphoric dream of his life, but no one responded to him. After a few minutes, one of the doctors told him to sign some discharge papers that the doctor said he forgot to have him sign before the procedure. Ali responded by telling the doctor he had already signed these forms prior to the anesthesia, but they insisted that he sign these additional forms, which he never received.

He jabbered on and on about this "dream" as they were driving away from the hospital, until finally his brother and cousin interrupted and said that they needed to tell him something. They proceeded to explain to him how his heart had stopped while he was under anesthesia and that he had been clinically dead for about two minutes. They told him how his eyes were open, and pupils fixated, and one last shot of the paddles had finally brought him back. One strange event that they witnessed was Ali's verbal communication right after waking up. Ali does not speak fluent Arabic and by no means speaks standard Arabic which is written and spoken in his Islamic faith, the *Holy Quran*. Both Ali's brother and his cousin were very amazed how Ali woke up speaking fluent Arabic as he recited verses and prayers from the *Quran* in standard Arabic. Once Ali was told that his heart stopped, and he was dead for about two minutes, he began to question his dream, his experience. After doing research, he concluded that his experience was not a dream but an actual out of body experience. Ali truly believes that his soul actually traveled through God's Heaven, but it was not time for him to make it permanent.

Ali told me that he now has absolutely no fear of death, and that he also has a whole new perspective on life here on earth. He no longer feels sad about death because, assuming that a person has a good heart, they will be in a better place when they die on earth. Last year, Ali's aunt passed away after a battle with cancer. When he heard, Ali smiled, gave her a blessing and said to himself, "*We will connect one day, you are in a much better place.*" Prior to his Dubai experience, Ali said he would have been sad and possibly cried.

Also, prior to his trip, he had been contemplating a joint business venture that he was not real sure about, but after his experience, he had all the confidence and trust in himself to move forward with it enthusiastically. It was a life-changing experience to leave his body for a short time, and I could tell he really struggled to describe it to me with mere words. It inspired me to write this:

Out in the Cosmos

Somewhere out in the cosmos way up high
In a place that I dreamed of under a velvet sky
Somewhere out in the cosmos life is true
And the sights that you long to see will appear to you

Someday I'll take a magic flight
And wake up with a white light
All around me
Where pain will melt like ice cream cones
Away up high on sailing thrones
That's where you'll find me

Somewhere out in the cosmos spirits fly
Souls fly out in the cosmos. When then, oh, when will I?

If blissful soaring spirits fly
Out in the cosmos when, oh, when will I?

I have also read books on after-life experiences written by mediums that I have found equally fascinating, and recently, my daughter bought me the book *Proof of Heaven* by Eben Alexander, M.D., for Father's Day. I read it during the time I took off from writing, which was soon after my mom passed away in 2015, and I completed it in only three sittings. I would recommend it for anyone who may be "on the fence" about the subject of life after death or grieving over the loss of a loved one. It is very compelling, to say the least, and also very inspiring—whether you believe in an afterlife or not. This time, immediately following the death of my mom, was the toughest time of my life since the loss of my dad in 2012, but my experiences with people such as Ali and Laurie, as well as reading *Proof of Heaven* and similar books, really helped to support my belief in the transition and survival of one's soul after death of the body. But the experience that had the most profound impact on bolstering this belief was when my dear friend, Donna, who is a psychic medium and energy worker, facilitated a session with me wherein both my mom's and dad's energies came through and personal messages were delivered to me. Donna had previously performed a similar session for my wife, Kim, wherein the energy of her deceased brother, Kevin, came through. Donna had never met my wife before, and Kim was astounded by the very personal information Donna conveyed to her and could not have possibly known about previously. Surprisingly, one of those messages involved information about one of my own brothers, which Kim and I knew to be true. This helped to validate the experience I had with Donna and the messages brought forth from Mom soon after her death. I felt a sense of calm and acceptance of Mom's and Dad's passings because I am convinced they still exist, although neither exist in the physical forms as I knew them.

"Life is pleasant. Death is peaceful. It's the transition that's troublesome."

– Isaac Asimov, American science fiction author and scholar (1920 - 1992)

Another book that I read many years ago was a biography about the life and death of Jim Morrison entitled, *No One Here Gets Out Alive*. The title to the book was taken from a Doors song, and it's a title that always sent a bit of a chill through my body. Earlier on, I described how I experienced some anxiety about the draft for the war in Viet Nam, and described that time of my life as "life on the killing floor." I may have dodged that particular bullet, but, as they say, "Something's going to get you eventually." Although I now know it is an unhealthy attitude to view the world as merely a waiting room to the funeral parlor, the title of the book inspired me to write this poem:

Harvest

Racing away on a runaway train
The ill-fated flight of Life
Through a one-way door, we're headed for,
The wrong end of the knife

Spiraling down the maelstrom of time
The great black hole of existence
A delicate cord, the gleam of His sword,
A warm bright glow in the distance

Riding the crest of life's big wave
This moment is to cherish, not to save
Time for laughter, time to weep
Why to sow if not to reap?

So plant the seeds of Wisdom, Love,
Happiness, and Sorrow
Deep into the heart of youth
The harvest of tomorrow

"The fear of death follows from the fear of life. A man who lives fully is prepared to die at any time."

~ Mark Twain, American novelist and humorist (1835 - 1910)

Of course, as I said, the best way I have found to go through life is with immense gratitude for all of the wonderful things and people in my life, and not to ever feel sorry for myself—at least not for any significant stretch of time. What I am *most* grateful for are all the kind and caring people who have helped me and supported me along my journey through this life. They are my biggest heroes and the ones whom I most aspire to emulate. One of the greatest joys in life is the feeling you get when you know you have helped another human being, even ones that you don't even know. That's what life is really all about.

The Mountain

There's a tall and mighty mountain
We're standing at its feet
By lurking in its shadow
We'll never see its peak

But its trails are cruel and heartless
And its perils never end
Sharp claws are there to greet you
'Round each and every bend

Climb forever onward
'Till you reach the peak
Tumble to dark valley
If the challenge you don't meet

Sometimes you'll feel it's hopeless
Futility may strike
But you'll have to find the courage
To complete your mortal hike

Climb forever onward
Hurdling the flames
This mountain can be conquered
Living is its name

It all ties back to the concept of living in the moment. Being in the here and now is like being in the only room in a big building where the lights are on. You can walk down the long hallway behind you into the past and be able to see for a while, but it will just keep getting darker and darker the further you go. The same goes for that hallway to the future that's in front of you. While we are alive here on earth, I believe this is vitally important—stay in the moment or you can get lost very easily. However, I also believe that beyond ordinary life here on earth—in the spirit world, if you will—the concept of time as we know it completely breaks down, as my friend Ali indicated when his two-minute ordeal seemed to last eighteen hours. In the spirit world, our souls may travel freely between the past, the present, and the future and the light shines brightly on all three. The following poem was inspired by William Shakespeare's *As You Like It, Act II, Scene VII [All the World's a Stage]*:

Show Time

The morning sun rises like a red velvet curtain
On the vast stage of life, where nothing is certain
The tragic, the comic, and the in-between
All a part of an endless scene
Where the sights and sounds of a million years
Touch our eyes and ring in our ears
There's cheer and hope, tears and pain
The scorching sun and the gentle rain

See the cast who light up the stage
The lover, the soldier, the fool, and the sage
Their curtain call, as twilight falls,
To bid us all farewell
The show must end
Our fate depends—
But only Time will tell

Time before and Time today
Swirl together and drift away
On a wayward morsel of Milky Way
Melting through a dream...

"Keep love in your heart. A life without it is like a sunless garden when the flowers are dead. The consciousness of loving and being loved brings a warmth and richness to life that nothing else can bring."

~ *Oscar Wilde*

CHAPTER SIX
THE WONDERS OF NATURE

"The goal of life is living in agreement with nature."

~ Zeno

It is now time to move on to a brighter subject, and one that is near and dear to my heart. Nature, in all its splendor and beauty, has captivated my soul since the days of my earliest childhood memories. Not just the wonders of nature here on our own earth, but those that traverse the entire universe. From the tiniest organisms to monolithic mountain ranges and throughout the vast expanse of outer space, there are infinite and timeless marvels that have the potential to fascinate us time and time again. That is, of course, if we only take the time to notice and *appreciate* all that nature has to offer us. It's so easy to get caught up in the minutiae of our daily lives that we often fail to recognize and enjoy even very simple pleasures that life has to offer, such as the warm sun on our bodies or a cool breeze on our face. It is through experiencing such plain, worldly sensations that we can come to know the divine.

Simple Secret

Living in a modern home
Have higher education
But wish that I would come to know
The secrets of Creation

Beneath a willow by the brook
I watched the waters flow
And caught a magic, fleeting glimpse
Of what I want to know

Gazing through the endless sky
I had a wondrous vision
Mother Nature kissed my eyes
And showed what I've been missing

You'll never find it in a school
Or any kind of temple
Look too hard and you're a fool
The truth in life is simple

I am very appreciative to both of my parents for instilling a reverence for nature in me. In their own individual ways, each would marvel at the miracles of life and nature. My mom was an animal lover, and she especially loved cats. While petting our family cat, she would often say to me how amazing it was to her that these creatures have eyes with which they could see and have feelings and ways of letting you know if they are hungry or want to be petted. Dad, on the other hand, was not quite the animal-lover type. In fact, he had a bumper sticker that read, "I love cats. They taste just like chicken!" After he passed, I had to keep it and still have it hanging up by my tool bench in my garage—the same place he kept it at his house. Although Dad didn't warm up to pets too easily, he could never resist *feeding* them. That was his soft-spot. He would never really show much affection for them like Mom, but I guess the Italian in him did like to see them enjoy a good chow. However, he did have a particular fondness for English bull dogs. He favored one himself, so it made sense.

Dad was more of the outdoors type who liked getting away to the mountains or the beach. He was also a big music lover, which is probably how I came to develop such an appreciation for all those beautiful compositions that have inspired me throughout the years. I remember that one of his favorite tunes was the old Louis Armstrong classic, *What a Wonderful World*. To this day, whenever I hear that beautiful melody, and even more beautiful lyrics, I think of Dad and feel a deep sense of gratitude for being exposed to the magic of music at such a young age. As I mentioned earlier, this had a profound impact on my view of the world and appreciation for all its wonders. I am sure that my dad really loved that song because he sincerely believed that this is such a truly wonderful world in which we live.

When I was a young boy, my parents would take us on family vacations up to New Hampshire where we would visit places such as Cannon Mountain in Franconia Notch State Park. Dad loved pointing out all the different features of the wilderness and snapping instant photos of us out in the wild on his trusty old Polaroid camera or filming us in motion on his Super 8. Franconia Notch is also known for some interesting rock formations, such as the Flume Gorge, the Lemon Squeezer, and the now-eroded Old Man of the Mountain, which we would always make sure to visit while we were up in that neck of the woods.

On one of those family trips up to Cannon Mountain, when I was about seven years old, I ran ahead of my family to the end of a trail that ended abruptly at a big rock cliff. My parents shouted for me to stop in obvious concern for my safety, so I complied. As they walked toward me, I noticed that there was a good-sized ledge about three feet down from the edge of the cliff where I stood. With a straight face, I waved goodbye to my family and jumped down to the ledge and smoothly crouched down in a single motion, so they wouldn't see any sign of me after the leap.

I can still remember the stunned, wide-eyed look on both my parents' faces as they gazed down over the edge of that cliff. The looks instantly changed to ones of simultaneous relief and annoyance when they saw me squatting down there with this mischievous grin on my face. "Get up here!" my dad barked. Later on in life, when I would inform my dad of stunts that my own kids pulled on me, he would revel in the stories with a big wide grin and say with delight, "Payback's a bitch"!

I mentioned earlier how my parents had sent me to a sleep-away camp up in the Catskill Mountains in New York when I was about eight years old. It was there that I first learned about things such as long hikes through the woods, camp fires, star-gazing, horse-back riding, sail boating, canoeing, and water-skiing. I am very grateful to have been fortunate enough to experience all those wonderful things at a very young age. To this day, my two sons and I make annual trips up to the north Georgia mountains to camp out for a few days and take in all that nature has to offer. I'm hoping they will pass that love of nature on to their own kids someday, the same way my parents passed it on to me.

"If the sight of the blue skies fills you with joy, if a blade of grass springing up in the fields has power to move you, if the simple things of nature have a message that you understand, rejoice, for your soul is alive."

~Eleonora Duse

Having spent all my childhood and most of my young adulthood on Long Island, I certainly spent more than my fair share of time hanging out at the beach. Most of the time, I visited one of the many sections of either Long Beach or Jones Beach, but some of my fondest memories are of the relatively few times I visited the beaches and small communities of Fire Island. While attending college at Oneonta, I met Adam Bernstein, AKA the

Burner, whose parents owned a summer home right near the beach in the Fire Island community of Saltaire. It is just east of the most westerly community on the island, which is called Kismet. There were two little bars in Kismet that were simply known as the Kismet Inn and The Out, which I believe are still there. Some of my college buddies and I would meet out there occasionally while visiting the Burner. What is really nice about Fire Island is that they do not allow any private vehicles on the island. They are extremely protective of the environment there, unlike most of the other more commercial beaches on Long Island. You had to get to Fire Island either by ferry boat from the mainland or by parking your car at the most easterly section of Robert Moses State Park and walking a few miles across the sand dunes until you finally arrive at Kismet. Being a young man in my early twenties and being used to doing a lot of hiking, I always opted for the latter mode of transportation. Those walks through the deserted and barren dunes also gave me good time to clear my head. No matter what beach, or what location, that same feeling followed me throughout the years. Whether on the beaches of New York, Florida, the Caribbean Islands or places such as Driftwood Beach on Jekyll Island, Georgia, the magic feeling followed me wherever I went.

There is just something about the beach that is hard for me to describe. No matter what is going on in my life, or how lousy a day or week I just had, all my problems just seem to dissipate in the salt air and drift away on the ocean breeze just like the seagulls hovering above.

Driftwood Beach, Jekyll Island, Georgia
Autumn 2015

Mystic Beach

Between the cities and the ocean's reach
There lies this warm and friendly beach
Where the eyes of the world consume the dawn
As the ocean rumbles its placid song

The sun cooks the sand to a golden brown
As the cool, rhythmic waves come
                                    tumbling
                                        down
Thoughts float like driftwood on the rolling surf
As sandcastle dreams melt to puddles of mirth

The beach has its ghosts and its ancient roots
It's been trodden by lovers and soldier's boots
A billion creatures there have perched
And found their souls without a search

After getting married in 1986, my wife and I decided to move to south Florida, so we could live near my sister and her husband, and also be close to all the nice beaches along the east coast of the sunny state. Being so close to the Florida Keys and the Caribbean Islands, the theme of pirates often cropped up in the course of our travels along Florida's east coast. Not to mention, a variety of tasty rum drinks, to which I took a liking, were also highly abundant and popular in that little corner of the world. The fondness that I acquired for consuming those sweet beverages and the "spirits" they contained dismayed my poor wife, who claimed I took on both the physical characteristics and offensive demeanor of a nasty old pirate whenever I consumed them. Between the swagger in my gate, the "lazy lid" in my left eye, and my raucous laughter and behavior, I eventually earned the moniker "Pirate Pauly." Of course, being dubbed with this nickname was nothing to be particularly proud of, but taking on that shameful persona did have one good side effect; it provided some inspiration for writing about a cursed old pirate vessel.

Ghost Ship

'Ship ahoy!' King Triton roared
A lifeless vessel, crew aboard
Ghost ship sails on ocean's spray
Her cold, damp prison
For God she betrayed

Unspoken vengeance therein lies
Bloated corpse with open eyes
Stubborn old captain blind with rage
Plowing his way through salty grave

Tormented shrieks, spine-chilling wails
Lightning thrashes her ghostly sails
Carrying tales too ghastly to tell
Riding a maelstrom bound for hell

Knowing what was good for me, I eventually heeded my wife's warnings to lay off the rum, but the nickname, and my love for the splendor and romance of beaches and the nautical landscape still live on strongly. Not only in the heat of day, but on into the dark of night, the attraction never fades. What better place is there to go star gazing than on a warm beach on a tranquil summer night? I recall sitting out along the shoreline of the Gulf of Mexico in Port Saint Joe, on Florida's Panhandle, after witnessing a spectacular sunset one such magical evening and becoming mesmerized by the orange flames of a mellow campfire that seemed to dance in rhythm with the soothing sounds of the nocturnal waves gently drumming across the sandy shore. I remember being spellbound as I looked up at the glittering night sky and saw millions of stars and constellations glistening in all directions like diamonds gracing a black velvet backdrop with their presence. And there, like a majestic silver curtain elegantly draped across the center of the whole sky, was the edge of our own mysterious galaxy—the Milky Way.

Long before that night and back when I was a young boy in elementary school, I remember my father taking me over to the adjacent middle school to look at the moon through a telescope that someone in the science department had set up. The moon looked so clear and close, I felt like I could touch it. At that time of my life, I had already taken up an interest in the space program and would even tell people I wanted to be an astronaut when I grew up. Now I was hooked! Besides building and shooting off model rockets, I would also spend time reading all about the stars, the planets, the solar system, galaxies, quasars, nebulae, black holes, and comets. As I got a little older, I became a big fan of the TV show *Star Trek* and imagined "going where no man has gone before." The study of astronomy is truly mind-boggling! Where does the universe end, or does it? Are there truly parallel universes, as suggested by modern day string theory? To this day, my love of the cosmos, and all its mysteries, has never left me— and never will.

Tiny Beach

There's a sea of stars and galaxies
Beyond our mortal reach
We sit down here and gaze at them
Upon our tiny beach

Wondering about eternity,
Infinity and life
The past and future holding hands
Like husband holding wife

Separate—remove yourself
Long enough to consider:
Who is that person staring me down
On the other side of the mirror?

And in the end, you'll justify
This really does make sense
How long can one just sit out there
Straddling the fence

Between life's known and the mysteries
Beyond the heavens' reach?
Until the day our ship pulls in
We'll comb our tiny beach

Before he passed away, I remember my dad telling me that *his* father had also taken up a deep interest in studying the cosmos but finally had to give it up because he found it just too overwhelming and perplexing. My grandfather, who I was named after, was a very intelligent man and a professor of linguistics at Brooklyn College in New York. He also coached the school basketball team. He died when I was very young, so I did not have the privilege of getting to know him very well or getting him to teach me any of those romance languages that he taught others. But from what I was told, and like a true scholar, he had a burning desire to see the "big picture" and figure out the meaning of all of existence. When you immerse yourself in something as vast and complex as the cosmos, along with all the different theories about time, space, relativity, quantum theory, and the like, it can really start getting to you. Evidently, poor old Doctor Salvatore had his mind blown trying to figure it all out! So, according to my dad, he just put it down and moved on. Guess he figured he would leave that sort of stuff up to guys like Albert Einstein, Carl Sagan, and Stephen Hawking!

Shooting Stars

Shooting Stars across the sky
Did you feel the magic high?
They burn like madness, fall and die
Shooting stars like you and I

Hear the music all around
Move in rhythm to the sound
Dance your feet into the ground
And snap the chains that have you

Bound to wake up, see the light
Moving swiftly, shining bright
Right is wrong and wrong is right
Shooting stars will fly tonight

Another season passes by
Still they make me wonder why
Shooting stars across the sky
Shooting stars like you and I

Similar to strolling along a beach, it is very easy to let your soul drift free while gazing out into a clear night sky and pondering the heavens and all of existence. What other life or civilizations may now exist out there, and how many countless others may have come and gone in the past? Have we ever been visited by any of them before, and do any still secretly visit us today? I marvel at the scientific notion that all of us are, in fact, related and made up of the same material that has existed for billions of years. Those materials originated out in the cosmos and were delivered to earth by projectiles that came from billions and trillions of miles away. Whether you believe that this was just a chance freak of nature or that it was by very deliberate divine design, it is still very awe-inspiring to contemplate "all that is" and the fact that we get to be a part of this great web of energy no matter how brief a period of time we have here on earth in relation to eternity. We will all eventually return to the universe, just as waves return to the sea, and still be part of it in some way, shape, or form.

Can Never Look Too Far

Living in a parody
Not lost but can't be found
Close that book on philosophy
And take a look around

Orchards under wind-swept trees
Airplanes over factories
Sand and sea that come together
Universe goes on forever

Ride your royal coach off through the end of the sky
Catch a glimpse of Heaven before it's time to die

And should your life be laced with pain
A twinkle in the eye remains
From gazing to the stars
You can never look too far

Contemplating the cosmos is great for helping to keep things in perspective, but another place of solace in which I find myself feeling a lot more grounded is out in the woods. Being around plants and trees has always had a very comforting effect on me, even if I just go for a short stroll out in the back yard. When I used to visit my maternal grandparents' home during childhood, I loved climbing up into a green apple tree they had on the property and just sit up there for hours on my favorite perch. I sometimes felt as if I had shapeshifted and became an extension of the branch on which I sat. Up there, I felt like I blended right in with nature and was able to get a birds-eye view of all my surroundings. Speaking of birds, Grandpa was also a big bird lover and built all kinds of bird feeders and nesting boxes that he mounted all around his very rustic property in the town of Babylon located out on eastern Long Island. When I would go out there to visit, he would bring me out to his work bench in the garage and teach me how to build them. This is a very rewarding craft that I still enjoy to this very day.

We humans often see ourselves as being superior creatures that dominate all other forms of life on earth. I have learned that all forms of life are equally amazing and share in the great web of energy that I referred to earlier. A bird, plant, tree, or even an insect is no less amazing to me as a human being when you look at them from the perspective that they are things that we ourselves cannot create. Yes, we can plant a seed, but can we make a seed? We could clone an animal, but could we create the cells we clone from? Even if we could produce such things, we could not make them grow. That would require help from the four elements of nature, including earth, air, water, and fire or sunlight. Some indigenous cultures also consider life-force energy, or spirit, to be an essential fifth element of everything in nature.

I would also dare to say that some creatures certainly have a whole lot more common sense and survival instincts than many humans do. Even plants, trees, and animals have the ability to adapt and survive in changing environments. If you think about it, a tree growing out of a crack in a rock on the side of a mountain could survive for many years through all four seasons without the ability to move and seek food or shelter. How long would a human survive out there with their foot stuck in the same crack? Some trees can even live for thousands of years. Although trees are bigger and stronger living organisms than us, many people callously look at them as just a big chunk of wood and wouldn't think twice about breaking out their chainsaws and clearing out their whole yard. I have learned to respect trees and understand that they produce the oxygen that we breathe. That means we can't survive without them, so we damn-well better respect them! They also provide food and shelter for many other forms of life in their respective native environments. And besides, who doesn't enjoy the view of a beautiful forest?

"Come forth into the light of things,
Let Nature be your teacher."

~William Wordsworth

During my college years in Oneonta, I liked to go for long hikes or jogs through the heavily forested hills that surrounded the campus. It was like instant therapy for me after long hard hours of classes and studying. The feeling of the wind on my face, and the combination of all the other sights, sounds, and smells throughout the wooded wonderland would bring me right back to reality and remind me that I am just another living, breathing creature of nature that dwells on our beautiful planet.

Along the route I took, there was a place called Table Rock that was a flat rocky area at the crest of a big hill that provided a breathtaking view of the valley below. This was a great spot to stop and meditate for a while. Another favorite spot of mine was a cliff that overlooked an algae pond deep in the woods on the side of a hill. Not only another great spot to sit and contemplate life for a while, but also to observe some other forms of wildlife such as frogs, salamanders, owls, and even a red fox or two. Last but not least, I also found a tall pine tree at the top of a hill that was great for climbing and reliving the days of my youth at Grandpa's house, but with a much better view. Watching a sunset ripen from any one of those places out in the woods would make my soul rise just like that of a kid who had just arrived at Disneyland.

Sunset Trail

Scattered sunlight through the trees
The path, like mine, meanders
A satin-soft pre-twilight breeze
Inspires contemplation

I thought about what's wrong and right
Like day and night that changes
My eyes reflected pastel lights
Of sunset gently waning

I swallowed down, to my soul,
The range of human passions
Feeling that my life is whole—
I only keep what matters

"You will find something more in woods than in books. Trees and stones will teach you that which you can never learn from masters."

~St. Bernard

Because of my love and appreciation for all of nature, I have always felt drawn to and respectful of people of Native American Indian culture. I share with them that same respect and reverence for our planet, the cosmos, and all living things that they have held true to for centuries. As a young boy, I remember seeing that commercial featuring a Native American man standing by the side of the road as some inconsiderate knuckle-head in a car passing by tosses a bag of trash out the car window that lands at his feet. Many people found that commercial to be a bit corny or even downright humorous—to see the tear running down the poor guy's face—but I always found it a bit disturbing. After all, why would people not want our one-and-only home planet to be pollution free? Clean air, clean water, clean earth that yields uncontaminated food to eat—that all sounds good to me!

I have a hard time understanding why people would be apathetic or indifferent to pollution, let alone vehemently fight against legislation that supports or mandates environmental responsibility. I understand that such legislation may cut into corporate profits, but what good will come from those profits if our quality of life is greatly diminished by pollution, or if the contamination and toxicity cause widespread illness and death? I've also noticed that many people are even cock-sure in their opinion that no matter what us humans throw at dear old Mother Earth, there's nothing we could possibly do to cause any real or meaningful damage to her. In my opinion, that is a destructive and irresponsible mentality that could end up spelling disaster for the human race, as well as many other species of life on our beloved planet, should this mindset persist. If bacterium were to have minds of their own and could speak, it would be like them asking each other, *"How can us tiny little bacterium possibly ever bring about the demise of a big old human being?"*

According to a report of the U.S. Global Change Research Program, "human activities, especially emissions of greenhouse gases, are the dominant cause of the observed warming since the mid-twentieth century." The report also documents how the destructive effects of climate change associated with global warming are expected to worsen if nothing is done to curb greenhouse gas emissions. Despite this clear, scientific evidence, there are still those who either ignore the findings or who direct their attention toward the potential ill effects on the economy if we address the problem. It truly amazes me how people can be more concerned about the economy when the very future of our planet and all life on it is being indisputably threatened.

In the summer of 2015, I was honored to be invited by my friend Bob Vetter to attend a Sun Dance ceremony held by Native Americans of the Southern Cheyenne and Arapaho tribes in the area of western Oklahoma. *The Encyclopedia of the Great Plains* defines Sun Dance as *"ritual ways of making local space sacred as a setting for renewal of the people's relationship with the land itself and with all the beings of their life-world, both human and other-than-human."* In simple terms, it is a very sacred ceremony that focuses on renewal of life—all life. Bob once told me that, in fact, there is a strong belief among those who participate in this ceremony that had they not held all the annual Sun Dance ceremonies in the past, our world and all life on it would have already perished. It humbled me to witness this event, and it made me so appreciative to know that there are still groups of such very proud and noble people living in our country who take the matter of survival of our planet and all living things as seriously and earnestly as they do.

I almost felt ashamed to be a white man present at such an event knowing just how far-removed this sacred way of perceiving nature is from the mainstream values—or lack thereof—that now seem prevalent in our country's "modern" culture. As a white man, I can only imagine the abuses that have been perpetrated against these astute and culture-rich people both historically and still today. The U.S. government is responsible for the deaths of millions of Native Americans, who were often viewed as merely nuisance creatures by the government since the arrival of European settlers in North America. Just one small example of this attempt at genocide was the Wounded Knee Massacre on December 29, 1890, during which five hundred U.S. cavalrymen surrounded and indiscriminately murdered 153 men, women, and children of the Lakota tribe and wounded thirty-three more. A total of eighteen officers and men who carried out this abomination were later awarded the Congressional Medal of Honor. To this day, those medals have never been rescinded.

Recently, the Black Lives Matter movement addresses the abuses of mostly young black people at the hands of law enforcement. Although it is true that young blacks aged twenty to twenty-four have statistically been the ones most likely to be killed by law enforcement in recent years at a rate of 7.1 percent per million of population, most people don't realize that Native Americans aged twenty-five to thirty-four rank a very close second at 6.6 percent per million of their respective population. Blacks in the same twenty-five to thirty-four-year-old age group are actually *less* likely to be killed by police as Native Americans. Overall, considering the percentage of the population, Native Americans are more likely to be killed by police than blacks. I strongly believe that we owe them a huge debt of gratitude, but the sad truth is this is how they are being "repaid" still to this day.

While traveling in Oklahoma, I had the pleasure of meeting a Native American couple, Wilbur and Melissa Goodblanket. I was saddened to learn that their eighteen-year old son, Mah-hi-vist, AKA Red Bird, was tragically killed by two law enforcement officers right inside their own home after his parents called for them to assist in a domestic disturbance. The dispute was "settled" when the officers shot their son seven times including once in the back of the head. According to Ma-hi-vist's girlfriend, Noami, who witnessed the shooting, Mah-hi-vist was unarmed at the time and was behaving calm and cooperative when he was gunned down in the family living room. The Goodblankets have been frustrated in their quest to seek justice for their son since the authorities refuse to release any evidence regarding the incident. To add insult to the tragedy, the two white Custer County Sheriff's deputies involved in the shooting were awarded the Medal of Honor and one the Purple Heart by his department just months after the incident. Sounds to me like history repeats itself—will the evidence ever be released to allow for a fair trial? Will *those* medals never be rescinded either?

At the close of the Sun Dance ceremony, I was heartbroken to watch Mah-hi-vist's mother stand and pray fervently at the altar in the center of the lodge after everyone except me had walked away. Praying seems like the only thing that one can do when the odds are so unfairly stacked against you. So, I prayed with her. In addition to praying for justice for her family and all those who have suffered similar injustice, I also prayed that one day all of mankind would show mutual respect for each other, as well as respect for all living things.

"When we show our respect for other living things, they respond with respect for us."

~Arapaho Proverb

Although praying is an important part of Native American culture, and partly because they had Christianity forced upon them by the "white man," I learned that their culture is based more on a strong belief in spirit as opposed to any particular set of religious dogma. They believe that all living things have a spirit, and therefore, treat all living things respectfully. For instance, while harvesting the wood used to construct the Sun Dance lodge, we first knelt and prayed and smoked a pipe in ceremony before a tribal elder, Moses Starr, Jr., took even the first swing of the axe at a tree. He later explained to me how he had spoken to the spirit of the tree and explained to it what we were going to do. This same respect is shown for animals and other living things that are killed for food. Often, gifts such as tobacco or sage are left as offerings in place of other plants that are harvested from the land. If you take something, you must give something. I dream of the day when this concept spreads to all of humanity. How wonderful would that be!

An Agreement with All Directions

Stars fall like snowflakes on dawn's horizon
Full moon riding on the crest of day
The world above and world below
Enveloping the world we know

Morning light of the vernal East
Heeds the teachings of the young
Like the yellow sun their wisdom shines
Never assuming what is right

From southern sky Red Bird will soon appear
A dear youthful spirit, trusting and innocent
Into the sacred summer waters he peers
Immune to the opinions of others

Insightful argonauts looking to the West
Never the settlers for second best
Warm in the womb of the black autumnal earth
Are endings—the Mother of all beginnings

Ancestral elders watching from the northern sky
Keeping an eye on winter's herd
Garbed in white, they come urging in the night
To always be true to your word

The Tree of Life gripping earth's core with its roots
Flowing through its trunk are endless vision questions
To the ends of the universe its branches reach
An agreement with all directions

It came as no surprise to me that Native American Indians also have a great sense of interconnectedness to all of nature, similar to the beliefs of Buddhism and other higher schools of thought. Besides honoring the four cardinal directions, they also honor the four seasons and the four basic elements—air, fire, earth, and water. They also recognize the existence of life-force energy—or spirit. Where most of us may look at something like a wooden chair and think of it as just a plain object that is separate from us, Native American belief recognizes that this is far from the truth. All four elements and spirit played a role in the existence of that chair, just as they do for our own existence. The wood from the chair came from a tree, which grew out of the earth. To grow, the tree required sun light (fire) and water. The tree took in carbon dioxide from the air and released oxygen back into our atmosphere—give and take. The chair was constructed by man, who breathes in air, requires warmth and water to survive, and whose bodies will one day return to the earth and whose life-force energy will return to the universe. So, you see, we really are all related and connected to each other and to all of nature in this great cosmic web that we each play a sacred role in.

"Humankind has not woven the web of life. We are but one thread within it. Whatever we do to the web, we do to ourselves. All things are bound together. All things connect."

~Chief Seattle

Ode to Big Bow

Falling gently on virgin plains
The silent sounds of summer rain
Here majestic creatures roam
The land Chief Big Bow calls his home

Spirit flows through Mother Nature, bringing Her to life
People sing and dance in rapture, purging all their strife
White men come in dark of night, Big Bow thinks them odd
Putting up a dreadful fight, but bearing books of God

Robes adorned with cross and moon
Road men will be coming soon
Down enchanted path of Love
Eagle soaring with the dove

Cleanse the air with cedar smoke and kindle tipi fire
Light the pipe and take a toke—Spirit rising higher
Owl Prophet with his mask, and sacred desert flower
Big Bow with a daunting task—Almighty healing Power

A new day dawns and they find themselves bound to a new nation
But Kiowa souls cannot be confined to any reservation
Oceans may turn to raging fires, and mountains turn to dust
Still we're all part of the universe, and it is part of us

*"Regard Heaven as your father, Earth as your Mother
and all things as your Brothers and Sisters."*

~Native American Proverb

From left to right, Robert Vetter, myself, Moses Starr, Jr. and his adoptive son Richie after the conclusion of the 2015 Southern Cheyenne/Arapaho Sun Dance in Oklahoma

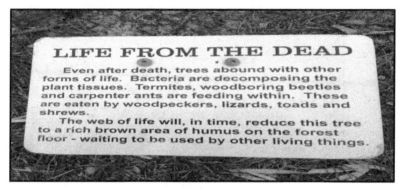

Sign posted at the T.H. Stone Memorial Saint Joseph Peninsula State Park near Port Saint Joe, Florida

For those who may think of the concepts of unity and interconnectedness as a bunch of philosophical bunkum appealing only to sentimental dreamers and bleeding-heart liberals who wish that we could all just get along, hold hands, and sing Kum Ba Yah—think again. There also happen to be very scientific and empirical examples of these concepts.

For one, there is a phenomenon in the field of quantum mechanics that is known as quantum entanglement. Albert Einstein supposedly referred to this concept as "spooky action at a distance" because even he could not explain it. The "spooky action" he was referring to is when two sub-atomic particles become entangled or connected to one another in such a way that if one of the particles is stimulated, it causes an equal and opposite reaction in the other particle. For instance, if one particle is made to rotate clockwise, the other particle would rotate counter-clockwise at the same rate, similar to a reflection in a mirror.

The truly amazing part of this theory of quantum entanglement of sub-atomic particles is that this interaction between the entangled particles would still occur even if the particles ended up millions of miles apart. Is it possible for information to travel faster than the speed of light between two particles, or is it that space is something that just gives the illusion of separation? Perhaps when scientists develop a more sophisticated understanding of this concept, we might be able to transmit information, or even ourselves, between galaxies almost instantaneously. Makes me wonder if there are other civilizations out there somewhere in our brave new universe that already have this concept all figured out.

Another example of interconnectedness in nature is in the world of trees. A local modern shaman and teacher of mine, Don Simmons, shared with me a video featuring Professor Suzanne Simard who gave a great presentation and explanation of this intriguing phenomenon in nature. From the Darwinian perspective, one would think that trees will tend to fight for position and strangle each other out in a fight for survival of the fittest where the bigger and stronger trees will win out. In reality, trees actually interact to help each other survive, and some of the larger trees play a bigger role in that process of helping other trees survive because of their extensive root systems. According to Professor Simard, carbon and nitrogen are exchanged between trees through complex underground root systems based on which ones need it. There is fungus in the earth that facilitates this exchange between the cortical cells of the roots. Even after some of those large trees are harvested by humans to use for lumber, this exchange continues to take place, and the roots of those harvested trees continue to pass on and share with the other trees whatever they have left in them.

"The needs of the many outweigh the needs of the few... Or the one"

~ from Star Trek – The Wrath of Khan

Although this sharing of resources comes naturally for trees out in nature, I couldn't help but make the observation that this is not always the case for all of humanity. Yes, there are many philanthropists and missionaries out there in the world, both rich and poor, who dedicate their lives to helping other people, and it comes very naturally to them. The word "hero" is very commonly applied to men and women of the military or public safety who sacrifice themselves in the line of duty, but those philanthropists and missionaries are real true heroes in my view as well. However, if it was suggested that this same concept of sharing resources the way trees do be a required way of life for all of *humanity*, many would immediately label it—in a derogatory manner—as left-wing liberalism, socialism, or communism. The standard outcry from those opposing this concept would surely be, *"But what about individual rights?"* Well, let's address that for a moment.

It is estimated that the top eighty richest people in the world have as much money as the least wealthy 3.5 billion people in the world, which is approximately half of the world's population. It is also approximated that the wealthiest one percent of the world's population has more wealth than all the rest of the world's population put together. Just let that sink in for a minute. Some think that this state of affairs is great, and others think that it is totally obscene and repugnant. Many others just really don't care either way or are blissfully unaware of these little "fun facts." My only comment is that this extreme situation of wealth inequality definitely sets off my yin-yang radar. The scales are tipped way out of balance, and it smacks of the classic, ongoing struggle of the bourgeoisie versus the proletariat, or the "haves" and the "have-nots," but to unprecedented proportions.

People seem to have become more and more mistrustful of government in recent decades. Don't think for a second that many of those massively wealthy people, or even big wealthy corporations, are not working hard behind the scenes to exert a great deal of pressure on all levels of government to promote legislation that will support their profit-making interests. In many instances, they represent that proverbial "man behind the curtain" who is pulling all the levers and acting as the mouthpiece for the big machine of government. Many of those interests are not consistent with the goal of maintaining a peaceful, healthy environment, including healthy people because implementing costly measures or regulations intended to protect the environment or our health can seriously cut into profit margins. There is the sad reality that many companies profit greatly from war, which is not so great for nature, either. I also find it unfortunate that some corporations profit from the practice of hording certain natural resources, such as drinking water, all around the world, thereby forcing people to have to buy it from them if they want access to this essential element of human life. However, I am glad to see that there are also a growing number of successful eco-friendly corporations popping up that promote the concept of "going green." I am particularly impressed with companies like Seventh Generation, which is a Burlington, Vermont-based company that produces environmentally friendly laundry detergent, trash bags, and diapers. Seventh Generation takes its name from an Iroquois law that says, *"In our every deliberation we must consider the impact of our decisions on the next seven generations."* Knowing there are organizations out there with this sort of responsible corporate mindset makes me feel that there really is some hope for the future. We just need a lot more corporations to follow suit.

There seems to be a big misconception in our country that the concepts of being economically responsible and being environmentally responsible are mutually exclusive. The notion is that we need to choose just one of these values and be on either one side of the fence or the other. Furthermore, our own government often promotes this misconception through political philosophy wherein Republican and conservative ideology generally supports policies that stress economic responsibility while the Democratic and liberal agenda focuses more on environmental responsibility, as mentioned in Chapter Four. However, as proven by a growing number of eco-friendly corporations, including huge corporations that develop and promote clean and renewable energy sources and green initiatives, conservation-oriented business endeavors can be quite lucrative and economically beneficial. Furthermore, there is no need for the government to step in and impose costly regulations to curb pollution when there is no environmental impact to keep in check. Undoubtedly, though, the efforts of lobbyists who support the deep-pocketed oil and coal industries want to perpetuate this misconception and political debate for as long as possible to protect their own financial interests. Therefore, it is up to "we the people" to think for ourselves, avoid this political quagmire, and make responsible choices as consumers. Then, it will naturally follow that the environmentally responsible companies receiving the economic support from consumers will thrive, while the others will falter and wane.

The important thing is that we all work together, no matter what our political inclinations or financial means, to protect and preserve the precious natural resources of our planet that sustain life. It is not like we can just move to another planet if the earth eventually becomes uninhabitable. Trees are being harvested at an alarming rate, and the list of attacks against our environment is far too extensive to elaborate on here. The point is, if we respect the earth, it will respect us. Conversely, nature has a way of fighting back and finding a way to survive. Think of the defensive way that white blood cells will gang up on threats within our own bodies. Mother Earth may one day decide to hack up the whole human race and spit us out like some sort of toxic hairball if we don't wake up and learn to respect her more.

"This is the way the world ends/not with a bang but a whimper."

~ T.S. Eliot

My dream is to one day see all the people of this world, especially those in government and big business, wake up and realize that we are running out of time for effectively dealing with the job of cleaning up the mess we have made. It is up to all of us to do our own little part to help make a difference, whether by planting some trees, cutting back on use of dangerous chemicals in and around our homes, conserving on energy use, donating to nature-friendly organizations, writing local politicians, or banning products or companies that are hurting our environment. What we do to our planet, we do to all of humanity and all living things. So please do something good, and if you ever find yourself gazing off into a feature of nature—whether it is the sky, an ocean, the woods or even the eyes of another living creature—and suddenly feel a profound sense of connection to everything your senses perceive, don't be surprised. It is because you *are* indeed linked to all of it. So, rejoice at the wonder of it all, and remember to be grateful and give back to this wonderful planet that gives so much to us!

"One touch of nature makes the whole world kin."

~ William Shakespeare

EPILOGUE
BRAVE NEW UNIVERSE

One thing we never have to worry about in this life is ever having a lack of topics to which we are exposed that fan the flames of human passion. In this book, I delved into topics such as time, mortality, philosophy, religion, politics, and a whole host of societal and environmental issues that certainly hit some sort of a nerve in all of us. For those who might say that they are not at all moved by any of these topics, I would have to question whether or not they are being completely honest with themselves, or if they have become desensitized in some way, for whatever reason. My assumption is that those who are the most extreme in their views, whether liberal or conservative; Republican or Democrat; religious or atheist; gun enthusiasts or gun controllers; pro environment or pro corporate profit without government interference; are the ones who are so passionate about these things that they probably didn't get through this whole book without tossing it in a trash can or a fireplace prior to finishing it. It was not my intent to insult or upset anyone with my opinions, views, comments, or the questions raised. These were just topics that unfolded a certain way for me in my own life and inspired me to express my feelings about them in the form of poems.

You may have noticed that one concept that I stressed throughout this book was balance. Since ancient times, this primal concept has been underscored in many schools of philosophical thought and belief systems. I also emphasized the importance of the greater good of humanity over that of the individual. Again, this is nothing new. Just read up on the Aristotelian philosophy of the Golden Mean and all these concepts are right there. Considering how long the basic tenets of moderation, balance, and the greater good have persisted all across the globe over centuries and millennium of time, it saddens me to think that we still have such a long way to go.

Another expression that my friend Bob once uttered with mischievous intonation was, "Everything in moderation, including extremes." This was back in our college days when he was alluding to how it is sometimes okay to go out and have a wild time, so long as you don't make a bad habit of doing so very often. I fully understood that point, but the expression still stuck with me in a way that had much broader meaning and application as the years unfolded. For instance, sometimes you have to work excessively hard, risking both mental and physical health, just to get an important job done. Likewise, you might find the need to goof off excessively and relax to the point of irresponsibility after those times that you know you pushed yourself way too hard. We need to be very conscious of those times and be careful to keep them in check and only let them happen in moderation.

I mention this because these same principles of balance and moderation can be applied to any and all of the topics explored in this book. Recall how I admitted to being a young liberal-minded punk who used to argue with my conservative father over political issues, but how that changed when I began working out in the "real world" where there are no "easy buttons." The less flexible and adaptable people are to different or changing situations in this world, the less likely it is that they will be capable of effectively coping with those situations. They might also find that the ritual of persistently clinging to their rigid or *extreme* views might cause them to become progressively more frustrated and judgmental, or even be reduced to counterproductive name-calling. Have you ever found yourself referring to someone as an "idiot" if they don't share the same view as you over gun control, or dismissing someone as an "ignorant moron" if they don't share the same views as you when it to comes to topics such as prayer in schools, immigration, politics, birth control, or the Ten Commandments in a court house? Have you ever been on the receiving end of such derogatory or inflammatory comments and called a fascist, hater, *libtard*, or snowflake?

No good could ever come from such quarrels without there being some form of moderation or attempt to understand each of the opposing views. On one end of the spectrum is respectful, cordial, and healthy debate that leads to some sort of compromise or understanding—even if you agree to disagree—and on the other end of the spectrum is possible violence or death. The latter really hits home with me when I think of those images of people in other countries burning the American flag and shouting, "Death to Americans," or even our own citizens, such as neo-Nazis and those street corner preachers I described in Minneapolis, who believe that any particular group of people should be annihilated for not looking or thinking like they do.

Instead of being dragged down to the level of name-calling or worse, it is wise to resolve oneself not to take such comments personally and try to understand that the words and actions of others are just a reflection of their own personal version or perception of reality; not necessarily *true* reality. As I've said, the opinions expressed in my writings are the result of how events unfolded for me in my own life. As a result, no one should take any of those things I wrote personally and get upset by them. I might not have even lived to write about it had I allowed those guys in Minneapolis shouting, "Death to white people," to get under my skin to the point it escalated to physical violence. Don't ever be senselessly robbed of your bliss and let other people move your energy to such a negative place where you feel compelled to lash out violently in reaction to their words and beliefs.

Some of my views throughout this book may have even seemed hypocritical or conflicting, and maybe some actually are, but it was the *passion* behind those topics that inspired me to write my poems. As I mentioned at the beginning of this book, passion and rationality don't always mix so well, and I have the humility to admit that I am far from perfect and am ignorant of many things. As much as we can possibly absorb in our relatively short lifetimes, we can still only scratch the surface of all there is to know. I am no longer that know-it-all college punk I used to be. The wiser we become, the more we understand how little we really know.

Hence, I have found it best if we just think for ourselves and resist becoming upset or manipulated by the opinions or comments of others. It is also important that we always try to keep an open mind and *truly* listen. We should use our own intuition, and perceive the world and people in it with understanding and compassion in our hearts, even if we view things completely different from those with whom we interact. We should not be too quick to make assumptions or jump to conclusions based on what we initially see or hear on the surface. Recall the empty cup and tinted glasses analogies. We will never be able to truly understand or peacefully coexist with others if we don't at least suspend our own beliefs long enough to catch the true essence of what someone else is trying to say. A wise Cree medicine man once taught me that we have two ears but only one tongue because we are supposed to listen *at least* twice as much as we speak. We still have free will to think and do as we please, but may come to find that the world does not necessarily need to be so contentious and belligerent if we adopt this "silent," tolerant, and open-minded approach. Expect to feel liberated and happier once loosening your grip on ways in which you may have rigidly conformed in the past. Let your religion be love and kindness and let your heart be filled with peace and tranquility.

When I wrote about human mortality earlier, one important point that was not explicitly stated is that death is the great equalizer. Whether you are religious and believe that our spirits will eventually all become part of the same divine light or an atheist who believes we will all become part of the same dust of the earth, there will still be an epic leveling of the playing field—either way. The one-percenter billionaires of the world will have nothing on the millions of homeless paupers. The powerful will have nothing on the meek; geniuses will have nothing on the mentally deficient; and members of no one race, creed, or nationality will dominate those of any others. Imagine humanity coming anywhere near that state of existence while we're all still alive! That's exactly what I imagined when I wrote the line, *"Catch a glimpse of Heaven before it's time to die,"* in the poem "Can Never Look Too Far" in Chapter Six. We can choose to expedite the process of coming together in this lifetime, or just wait a few thousand more years.

Assuming mankind still exists a few thousand years from now. Whether we all go in a flash from an asteroid or nuclear strike, or die a slow painful death from failing to respect our host planet, we will still leave our legacy if things don't change. In the poem "The Mirror" in Chapter Four, the final line foretells, *"The way we treat each other will reflect the human race."* How sad would it be if explorers from other planets ever discover our earth after we are all gone and all they find is evidence of thousands of years of warfare, environmental destruction, and conflict? Perhaps we are already the subject of their pity?

The way I see it, there are basically three kinds of people in this world who have existed throughout the history of mankind. First, there are the people who want to divide and conquer. They are often driven by fear, greed, or both and want to control, manipulate, and dominate the world around them, including other people, the physical environment, and perhaps all other resources and creatures. Although these people represent a minority of the population, they are the ones who wield great power and authority in society, particularly in many governments, certain religious institutions, and big business.

At the other extreme, there are people who simply want to live in harmony with their fellow man and all of nature; those enlightened beings with love and kindness in their hearts who not only want to help and support other people, animals, and the physical environment, but actually find pleasure in doing so and are truly grateful for all they are blessed with here on this beautiful planet. These people may be very wealthy or not have a penny to their name. Unfortunately, these beautiful souls seem to be in the minority as well.

In between these two extremes, lies the third type. They are the masses of people who tend to show moderate qualities of both these extremes depending on their situation at any particular time, but who basically just want to "live and let live." Their main goal is simply to survive and move forward day-to-day, week-to-week, month-to-month, and year-to-year focusing on providing food, shelter, clothing, and perhaps a good education for themselves and their families and not concerning themselves very much with what is happening in the rest of the world, including the affairs of people of the two minority extremes.

Therefore, I believe the *majority* of people in this world are good people who just want to live out their lives and enjoy all life has to offer the best they can. Why, then, are there so many problems in the world? Although I strive to be nonjudgmental, if I were forced to pick and choose who to blame for those problems, my initial knee-jerk reaction would probably be to blame the first minority—the controlling power-mongers of the world who have forced their will upon the masses. From my observations, they seem to be the ones who have fostered the passionate emotions associated with religion and nationality over the course of history. They also appear to be the ones who have instilled fear in the masses for not showing loyalty to, or conforming and complying with, the laws and rules of nation and religion, thus exercising great influence and control over the masses. Similar to the futuristic scenario described in *Brave New World* and societies controlled by dictators over the course of history, when people are born into such a controlled environment and these customs and beliefs are all they are exposed to their whole life, the stranglehold of power and control is seemingly unbreakable.

However, there is another side of me that also tends to place blame on the masses of people in the majority group described above because of qualities such as apathy to important issues, irresponsibility or immoral behavior, abuse of rights and privileges granted to us by the government, and other exhibition of behavior that would make a governing body or other rulers feel it is imperative to take strong action to maintain stability in society. These qualities are exactly what brought about the scenario of the tightly controlled social order depicted in Huxley's *Brave New World*. Therefore, I ultimately see it as one of those "chicken or the egg" situations where blame can be placed on either group, or on neither.

I have concluded, therefore, that it is completely up to those of us in the world who have the freedom to read, write, and think for ourselves to study and understand how history has unfolded so that we might better understand, accept, and peacefully coexist with our fellow man. It is also incumbent upon us to behave responsibly and not give our leaders reason to feel it is necessary for them to maintain order by restricting our individuality and freedoms. It is important for us to stand up and take action when leadership *does* seem to be overreaching in their power with attempts to unjustly control us. If it is evident that taking action against the abusive leadership is futile, the next best option is to refuse to participate in it. For example, when the ruthless dictator Adolf Hitler started rising to power in Germany, my grandfather fled the country and family he so dearly loved to seek refuge here in the United States. Similarly, centuries prior to that, countless Europeans left their respective countries seeking freedom from other undesirable conditions, such as religious persecution and also crossed the ocean seeking refuge in North America. Naturally, people are leery of such uninvited refugees barging into the portion of this planet that they currently occupy and dominate, so the immigrants are not always welcome and greeted with open arms. However, not all the settlers that came across the ocean were a threat to the indigenous natives of North America and, in fact, many would have perished if the indigenous people had not come to their aid and helped them to survive. As evidenced by the first Thanksgiving in 1621, as well as the relationships that pacifist Quaker William Penn developed with Native Americans, history has shown that many of those early settlers were grateful to the natives and made a sincere effort to peacefully coexist with them. Some even married Native Americans and raised families with them. But along with those settlers who displayed a "live and let live" mindset, there were those who were fearful and greedy. Although these power-mongers came seeking freedom from oppression themselves, it was not enough for them to live and let live on the newly discovered continent; they needed to keep forging west in a quest to own and control as much as they could, just as conquerors throughout Europe and Asia had done for centuries before them. But are all Germans bad because of Hitler and are all Americans bad because of General Custer, Andrew Jackson, and the like? Our passions might tell us "yes," but our reason should tell us "no."

Although the power-mongers of society may sit in a strong position of control, it is important to keep in mind that they are vastly outnumbered, or, as Jim Morrison put it, *"They got the guns but we got the numbers."* Therefore, I advocate that the masses of common people rise up and make a stand in their own peaceful and productive way. I admire and encourage those who take some form of meaningful action to defend and support what they believe in. Don't expect change without the will to take action.

"The good inside of all of us is wrapped in a layer of apathy, and we forget how much potential we have within us, in each and every one of us, to change the world for the better for ourselves and our children, and thus to bring about oneness."

~ Shari Arison

Finally, I would like to emphasize the importance of, and the *power* behind, the act of setting intentions. This act pertains to all the topics and concepts discussed in this book, such as bliss versus despondence, love versus fear, freedom versus responsibility, and negative versus positive thoughts, to name a few. When you successfully combine the concepts of moderation and balance with the act of setting very deliberate good intentions that serve both your *highest* self *and* the greater good of all, you will understand just how quickly you can effect positive change. If we all made a sincere pact to humbly and respectfully do our personal best to make ourselves and our world a better place for *all* to live, including all of nature, then it simply *will* be. There's a brave new universe waiting out there for all of us to enjoy *together.* Let's not wait any longer.

Brave New Universe

Poets, shamans, great musicians
Psycho artists, soul beauticians
Peace and war, man's devices
All his virtues and his vices
Will come together—crystalize—
When wisdom melts deep-frozen eyes

Behind the doors of Billy Blake
King of Lizards rides the snake
Out to wander, out to pasture
Until the soul becomes the master
Mighty mountains, raging rivers
All the things that life delivers

Invoke great spirits, sail adrift
Flaming arrows screaming swift
Earth-walk; brief, amazing stroll
Toward the light red carpet roll
Thoreau and Nietzsche, Jesus, too
On the other side will meet you

Free-way leads to higher knowledge
Past the churches, schools, and college
Across the oceans, through the sky
Like the shooting stars we fly
Labyrinth of life, so shall we solve
When toward the light, our souls evolve

Veiled by mysterious silver curtain
What lies beyond is not for certain
But Midnight Hawk and the sacred seven
Still plot a course to visit Heaven
Climb aboard and together we'll traverse
The span of our brave new universe

THE END

THANK YOU

Thank you for taking the time to read *Brave New Universe*. If you enjoyed it, please consider posting a short review on the retail site where you purchased it. Reviews are very helpful to all authors. Also, tell your friends about it. Word of mouth is an author's best friend and much appreciated. Again, thank you.

~ Paul J. Salvatore

RESOURCES

Help Nature

National Audubon Society - http://www.audubon.org/
National Parks Foundation - https://www.nationalparks.org/
National Wildlife Federation – www.nwf.org
The Nature Conservancy - https://www.nature.org/
World Wildlife Fund – http://wwf.panda.org/
Defenders of Wildlife – www.defenders.org
Environmental Career Opportunities -
    https://www.cnbc.com/2017/04/20/9-great-jobs-for-
    people-who-want-to-save-the-planet.html
Ways to Help the Planet - http://www.50waystohelp.com/

Charities

The Life You Can Save - https://www.thelifeyoucansave.org/
Give Well - https://www.givewell.org/
Charity Navigator - https://www.charitynavigator.org/

Self-Help and Inspiration

Oneness: Great Principles Shared by All Religions – Jeffrey
    Moses - http://onenessonline.com/
Mysticism Information– Graham V. Ledgerwood -
    http://themystic.org/index.htm
Adam Bernstein – medium - Between the Worlds –
    http://www.adambetweentheworlds.com/media/
Don Simmons – shaman, psychic, healer - The Mystic Path -
    http://www.themysticpath.com/1.html
Donna Shafer – psychic, medium, healer - Energy Life

Movement – elmspiritoftrees@gmail.com
Robert Vetter – anthropologist, educator, healer -
   https://www.indianjourneys.com/
Laura Davis and Andrea Harvey – artists –
   www.lauramariedavis.com

REFERENCES

Adams, Susan. "11 Companies Considered Best for the Environment," Forbes, April 22, 2014.

Alexander, M.D., Eben. *Proof of Heaven*. New York: Simon & Schuster, 2012.

Alpert, Dr. Richard into Baba Ram Dass. *Be Here Now*. San Cristobal, New Mexico: Lama Foundation, 1971. Hanuman Foundation, 1977.

Barnes, Ian. *The Historical Atlas of Native Americans*. New York: Chartwell Books, 2015.

Boyle, Philip. "Public Problems, Values and Choices," *Popular Government*, Fall 2001.

Byrne, Rhonda. *The Secret*. New York: Atria Books, 2006.

Capra, Fritjof. *The Tao of Physics*. Boulder, Colorado: Shambhala Publications, 1976.

Centers for Disease Control & Prevention, National Center for Health Statistics, Center on Juvenile & Criminal Justice. "Rate of Law Enforcement Killings, per million population per year, 1999 – 2011."

Cohen, Ken. "Native Wisdom: Seven Keys to Health & Happiness," *Sounds True*, 2003.

DeCaro, Peter F. *Along the Way*. New York: Invictus Press, 1980.

Einstein A, Podolsky B, Rosen N; Podolsky; Rosen (1935). "Can Quantum-Mechanical Description of Physical Reality Be Considered Complete?" Phys. Rev. **47** (10): 777–780.

Engelsiepen, Jane. "Mother Trees" Use Fungal Communication Systems to Preserve Forests, Ecology Webinar Series, October 8, 2012. http://www.ecology.com/2012/10/08/trees-communicate/.

Evans, Dr. Tony. Let's Get to Know Each Other. Thomas Nelson Publishers, 1995.

Fowler, Jeaneane. *An Introduction to the Philosophy and Religion of Taoism*. Sussex Academic Press, 2005.

Hopkins, Jerry and Danny Sugerman. *No One Here Gets Out Alive*. Plexus Publishing, 1980.

Huxley, Aldous. *The Doors of Perception and Heaven and Hell*. Harper & Brothers, 1954, 1956.

Huxley, Aldous. *Brave New World*. Harper & Brothers, 1932.

Jones, Andrew Zimmerman and Daniel Robbins. *The Basic Elements of String Theory (from String Theory for Dummies)*. Hoboken, New Jersey: Wiley Publishing, Inc., 2010.

Laertius, Diogenes. *Lives of Eminent Philosophers*, Volume 1, Books 1-5. Loeb Classical Library, No. 184, 1925.

Lee, Bruce. *Tao of Jeet Kune Do*. Burbank, California: Ohara Publications, Inc., Linda Lee, 1975.

Madden, Thomas F. "The Real History of the Crusades," *Crisis Magazine*, March 19, 2011.

Malhotra, Ashok K. "Sartre's Existentialism in *Nausea* and *Being and Nothingness*." Lake

Gardens, Calcutta, India: Writers Workshop, P. Lai, 1976.

Moses, Jeffrey. *Oneness: Great Principle Shared by All Religions*. Ballantine Books, October 29, 2002.

Moya-Smith, Simon. "Who's Most Likely to be Killed by Police?" Commentary featured on CNN, Wednesday December 24, 2014.

Pearl, Mathew. "Faith Brings Together Riders of Different Races After Charleston Shooting, September 13, 2015," WXIA-TV, Atlanta.
http://www.11alive.com/story/news/local/features/2015/09/1

3/faith-brings-together-riders-different-races-after-charleston-shooting/72220638/

Ruiz, Miguel. *The Four Agreements*. San Rafael, California: Amber-Allen Publishing, Inc., 1997.

Sagan, Carl. *The Dragons of Eden*. New York: Ballantine Books, The Random House Publishing Group, Random House, Inc., 1977.

Singer, Michael A. *The Untethered Soul*. Oakland, California: New Harbinger Publications, Inc., 2007.

Snider, Daniel Dee. *Shut Up and Give Me the Mic*. New York: Gallery Books, 2012.

Stern, Mark Joseph. "Oklahoma Tea Party Candidate Supports Stoning Gay People to Death, Slate, Outward, Expanding the LGBTQ Conversation," June 11, 2014, The Slate Group, http://www.slate.com/blogs/outward/2014/06/11/oklahoma_tea_party_candidate_scott_esk_supports_stoning_gay_people_to_death.html

Stevens, Jose and Lena and the Philip Lief Group, Inc. *Secrets of Shamanism*. New York: Avon Books, 1988.

The Winning Life – An Introduction to Buddhist Practice. Santa Monica, California: World Tribune Press, 2007.

Trainor, Kevin. *The Illustrated Guide of Buddhism*. Oxford University Press, 2004.

Tzu, Lao. *The Way of Life*. New York: Capricorn Books Edition, 1962.

USGCRP, 2017. *Climate Science Special Report: Fourth National Climate Assessment, Volume I* [Wuebbles, D.J., D.W. Fahey, K.A. Hibbard, D.J. Dokken, B.C. Stewart, and T.K. Maycock (eds.)]. U.S. Global Change Research Program, Washington, DC.

Vetter, Robert and Richard Tartsah, Sr. *Big Bow: The Spiritual Life and Teachings of a Kiowa Family*. Eastport, New York: World Journeys Publishing, LLC, 2012.

Walker, Jade. "Richest 1 Percent to Own More than Half of the World's Wealth by 2016, Oxfam Finds," The Huffington Post, November 10, 2015.

Wishart, David J., Editor. *Encyclopedia of the Great Plains.* University of Nebraska Press, annotated edition, 2004.

ABOUT THE AUTHOR

Paul J. Salvatore was born in Brooklyn, New York, and grew up on Long Island. Ever since his days in college, he's enjoyed exploring the spiritual aspects of existence as he questioned his own religious instruction. His career as a public servant in the field of government finance is one aspect of his life, but his search for meaning in *All That Is* led him down many paths. His book, *Brave New Universe,* explores what he has discovered along the way. From extensive studies to visiting Native American tribes and experiencing their quest for truth, he's learned what really matters in this life and beyond. He hopes to impart some of that knowledge to others, so the world has a chance of becoming a better place.